Plan to Not Pay Taxes

PLAN TO NOT PAY TAXES

TAX FREE ACTIVE INVESTING STRATEGIES

Chris Koomey

CONTENTS

Foreword

Planning is not something that a majority of people get excited about. Despite great quotes like "Failing to Plan is Planning to Fail" and the like, I realize that people who like to plan are a minority in the population. I think part of the problem is that thinking years and decades ahead when it comes to financial planning is so far removed from the here and now it is hard for people to get excited about it.

Through this book, <u>Plan to Not Pay Taxes: Tax Free Investing Strategies</u>, I am hoping to get you excited - excited about planning to not pay taxes. The goal of this book is to get you to realize the immense opportunity you have to plan to live a tax free life. In this book, I will show you how to:

- Plan to Not Pay Taxes for up to Half of Your Adult Life
- Incorporate Active Investing Strategies Into Your Success Plan
- Implement 6 Strategies for using the Last US Tax Haven
- Execute 5 Business Models with Your Tax Free Strategies
- Build Up Sufficient Capital to Finance Several Tax Free Strategies to Fund the Rest of Your Life
- Leave a Tax Free Legacy for Future Generations

This book is for those of you who hate paying taxes or just want to better understand the rules so you can benefit from the Best Business in the World: Tax Free Active Investing.

PREFACE

"Business is hard. That's why you need a Business Godfather." This is a saying you'll hear me use a lot. Because it's at the core of what the Business Godfather is all about. I love working with businesses. As a successful entrepreneur, I know first hand how difficult growing businesses can be. I work and consult with growing businesses from startups to large corporations to help them become more valuable and achieve their strategic objectives.

I started my first business when I was 19 and since then I have opened up businesses and helped others open up and grow business as a business owner, business consultant and business attorney. I graduated from the Marshall Wythe School of Law at the College of William and Mary after receiving BA & MA degrees from the University of Chicago and an MS degree from George

Mason University. Business Godfather, LLC was established in 2012 to bring together all the aspects of my experience and background.

The Business Services offered by the Business Godfather, LLC have been developed over the past two decades to help clients build more valuable businesses and achieve their strategic objectives. The Business Godfather, LLC is not associated, affiliated, sponsored or endorsed by Viacom, Inc., Paramount Pictures Corporation or any other entity associated with "The Godfather" book or movies which relate to the arts and entertainment industry. "The Godfather" trademark and associated intellectual property are owned by Paramount Pictures Corporation and Business Godfather, LLC makes no claim to ownership of intellectual property associated with "the Godfather." The Business Godfather, LLC is also not associated, affiliated, sponsored or endorsed by an international crime syndicate real, imagined or fictional.

CHAPTER 1

THE BEST BUSINESS IN THE WORLD

Back in my lawyer days, I had several clients come in and ask me how their business could be structured so they would not have to pay any taxes. "That's easy," I would tell them, "Just don't make any money!" I would explain they were looking at it all wrong that instead of not paying any taxes they should figure out how can they pay more taxes than anyone else because that meant they were making more money than anyone else. Now I understand that that's not exactly right but the point was to get people thinking productively about building their business rather than thinking about how they can step over dollars to pick up dimes.

Why did so many people think there was a way to run a successful business and not pay any taxes? This is primarily a vestige of the pre-1986 US tax code which

1

included high marginal tax rates but all sorts of deductions and ways to reduce taxable income through passive investments. Most of these opportunities were closed with the 1986 US tax code revision which lowered tax rates but also eliminated many non-economic uses of the tax code to benefit individuals. Depreciation and amortization schedules were standardized and lengthened. The ability to deduct passive losses has been limited. In the 30 intervening years, most of the holdover opportunities have been closed such as the small insurance company exemption from paying gains on investments and many others.

Your Uncle Sam has been pretty clear: for the most part if you generate income, your Uncle wants you to pay taxes.

At the same time, wouldn't it be great if you could build a business that would have a great impact on the world and provide you and your family with tax free income for the rest of your life? This sounds like a fantasy, but this is an achievable goal as part of your overall success plan with proper use of Roth Tax Free Vehicles. A tax free business could be the best business in the world for you.

Your benevolent Uncle has provided a clear method for you to generate tax free income through Roth IRAs and Roth 401Ks (Roth Tax Free Vehicles). Only individuals who are 59 1/2 or older can receive tax free income from these vehicles. However, everyone can start planning as to how they can take advantage of this incredibly powerful tax free income tool.

The Roth IRA and Roth 401K are incredibly underutilized. The Investment Company Institute states that only 8% of total IRA assets are held in Roth IRAs. https://www.ici.org/viewpoints/ci.view_14_ten_facts_roth.print

This is an amazing opportunity to generate tax free income that is being missed by the vast majority of investors. Even better, as a Business Owner you have the perspective and the experience which will allow you to get the greatest benefit from using Roth Tax Free Vehicles to generate tax free income.

There has been a massive bias in tax deferred and tax free investing in financial assets. There are many more lucrative options for investing beyond financial assets. Businesses that you are an Active Investor in are the best place for you to invest your capital in. Business owners' best investments have been in businesses, in real estate and in asset development. These are the opportunities that you will get the best return out of by using the Roth Tax Free Vehicles.

Successful business people generate multiple streams of income whether it is within a single business or through various business ventures. At a minimum, at least one of those streams of income should use a Roth Tax Free Vehicle to give you the opportunity to achieve the benefits of tax free income and estate planning.

This book is for individuals who are looking to develop tax free strategies as part of their long term business and wealth planning. This book is not for individuals who are looking for a quick fix, a short term tactic or a magic solution to all your problems. You need to be successful to make these strategies work for you. You need to have excess income to make these strategies work for you. You need to give yourself the opportunity to make these strategies work for you.

Success Planning

In <u>The Business Godfather Treatment</u>, I discuss how important Success Planning is for business owners. Success Planning is purpose driven financial planning. Your Success Plan is what you are trying to accomplish personally through your various business investments and your assets.

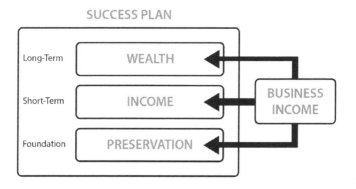

Your Success Plan is built on a foundation of Preservation. Basically, your preservation strategies are designed to give you peace of mind and allow you to sleep soundly at night. These are your "In Case of Emergency, Break Glass" Strategies. Generally these do not need to be generating significant returns and are generally low risk approaches to your assets.

Your Preservation Foundation supports Income Strategies and Wealth Building Strategies. Income Strategies are designed to meet your monthly income needs. Wealth Building Strategies are to develop assets to address any future goal you might have: e.g. retirement, education, legacy, etc.

My recommendation is that you have 3 Preservation Strategies, 3 Income Strategies and 3 Wealth Building Strategies operational at all times. You also may want to develop additional strategies in anticipation of individual strategies running through their useful life or as they pertain to how you want to focus your resources.

The Tax Free Strategies identified herein clearly start out as Wealth Building Strategies and may convert to Income or remain as Wealth Building Strategies. At a minimum, develop at least one tax free strategy. You may choose to develop multiple tax free wealth strategies.

Because I know that most people do not have significant assets positioned in Roth Tax Free Vehicles I will spend some time in Chapter 5 discussing how to build up sufficient assets to implement some of these strategies. If you already have significant assets positioned in Roth Tax Free Vehicles you can start implementing some of the strategies identified in Chapter 4 immediately.

Tax Free Active Investing

In this book, I will examine developing tax free business opportunities as part of your overall success plan. I will discuss the mechanics of the Roth Tax Free Vehicles and lay out a strategy to position your assets in a tax free manner. I will discuss business opportunities that will work using Roth Tax Free Vehicles.

In order to plan not to pay taxes effectively, you need to change your perspective on Roth Tax Free Vehicles. The Roth Tax Free Investment Vehicles are designed to provide you with Tax Free (or Tax Deferred) Investment Income. The restrictions on receiving direct benefits from your Roth Tax Free Investments are designed for this to be used for investments where you put your money in and get a return at a later date. There is nothing preventing your active participation in the investment; you just can't receive compensation for your services.

For many people, I realize this is a non-starter. Some people will only put in effort when they will receive current income compensation. The strategies outlined in this book are not for these people.

The strategies outlined in this book are for people who have their income covered through other means. These other means could be a salary, income from other businesses, cash flow from other investments, whatever. The strategies outlined in this book require planning and patience. They are also not singular strategies that you pursue to the exclusion of all other strategies. As a successful business owner, you should be looking to develop multiple streams of income. My proposition to you is that at least one of them should be via a Roth Tax Free Vehicle.

I generally advocate triangulating strategies where I have 3 strategies working to address the same goal. This diversifies opportunities and risk. The beauty of this approach is that if one of your strategies achieves your goal, things are great. But even where strategies are only partially successful, if all 3 provide positive results you may achieve your overall goal any way.

One of the barriers to successfully implementing the strategies outlined in this book is that the conventional financial services industry has subverted the power of Roth Tax Free Vehicles and other tax deferred vehicles such as IRAs and 401Ks to serve the purposes of their Passive Investment Model. The conventional financial services industry has so subverted and co-opted people's thinking about these vehicles that people have a deep seated resistance to doing anything other than Passive Investments.

Part of the subversion of Roth Tax Free Vehicles and tax deferred vehicles is that the financial services industry has gotten everyone to think of them as Passive Investment Vehicles. I understand for most people this is appropriate because research shows most people do not make effective financial decisions for themselves. But my appeal in this book is not for everyone but for people who have had success as Active Investors. People who have built successful businesses should be applying their experience and skills to their own capital so they can get a better return than relying on someone else. Even better, take advantage of the Roth Tax Free Vehicles and you can fund a tax free business for the rest of your life.

I was discussing the ideas in this book with a young 20 something entrepreneur and he immediately thought of money in a Roth Tax Free Vehicle as something for retirement. The financial services industry has done such a great job convincing you that your greatest financial asset is not accessible to you and you believe it.

If the conventional financial services Passive Investment Model were providing returns sufficient to support most people, then this would not be such a big deal. However, the Passive Model has been providing individuals with low single digit and even negative returns once fees and expenses are included in the calculation for most of the 21st century. On a consistent basis about 85% of mutual funds fail to beat the market index that they compare themselves to. Most hedge funds are failing to beat the market index as well. US growth is expected to be restrained for the next 15 years or so and growth fuels stock market returns. US individual stock ownership is at its lowest level recorded in decades. The financial services Passive Investment Model is in a state of crisis and does not appear to have a light at the end of the tunnel.

Corporate Communism versus Active Investing

Throughout the past 500 years of capitalist history, passive financial investments have not been the most successful vehicles to invest in. Passive investment vehicles have only risen to prominence in the past 30 years. The financial services industry marketing has been so effective that people overlook the past 15 years of mediocre returns.

The original capitalists were shopkeepers and traders who took advantage of market inefficiencies and created businesses that provided affordable products, which improved people's lives. Capital investments developed to take advantage of opportunities in global trade such as through the Dutch East India Company and the British East India Company and then on to resource acquisition opportunities such as whole ships and mining and then infrastructure opportunities such as railroads, airlines and telecommunications. For most of these 500 or so years, successful investment meant Active Investment as investors selected a Board of Directors who was responsible for active management of the company.

The past 30 years have flipped this model of Active Investing upside down and inside out. Originally, the board of directors of a company protected shareholders' interests but in this new anti-capitalist model the Board of Directors serves the interests of the managers. The managers controlling the means of production has been very destructive to the interests of investors and to capitalism as a whole. It didn't work in the Soviet Union and its not doing well for investors in publicly traded companies in the US.

Effectively, the financial services industry Passive Investment Model has you placing your hard earned capital into organizations managed on communist principles that have little regard for the providers of capital. I understand that these companies are said to be capitalist but if you remove what they say about themselves and focus on how capital is treated you will see the managers control the means of production and those providing capital do not get a return adequate to compensate them for the risk they are taking. I understand pure communism intended to devolve power to the individual worker, but communism in practice devolved power to the managers and their supporters and that is what the financial services Passive Financial Investment Model provides you with.

I am not trying to lead a revolution against corporate communism. My point is that putting your hard earned capital into them and expecting more than mediocre returns is not reasonable given their track record. You can use Passive Financial Investment as a preservation strategy but it is not a viable income or wealth strategy for most people. People that have bought into the Passive Financial Investment model used to target 10-12 % returns but now expectations are closer to 4-6 % and reality is more like 2-4% over the past 15 years.

If you want to invest in capitalist organizations you either need to elect an active Board of Directors who defends and promotes the interest of those who provide capital or be an Active Investor yourself. Farmers are the ultimate Active Investors as each season's planting is designed to capitalize on future market conditions. Farmers constantly develop multiple streams of income to help them hedge against market uncertainties. Self sufficiency coupled with market upside opportunities are the key to a successful farming operation and Active Investing strategy.

For most of the 500 years in the development of capitalism, Active Investors have been the ones to reap the greatest rewards. Even now as you look at the list of the world's richest people, they developed their wealth primarily through Active Investing in businesses or real estate. My bet is this is the same for you as well. It's time for you to put all your assets under an Active Investing approach.

CHAPTER 2

POLISHING YOUR WEALTH DIAMOND

There are four basic ways that you can hold assets in the US: Cash or Cash Equivalents, Taxable Investments, Tax Deferred Investments and Tax Free Investments. I developed the Wealth Diamond several years ago so people can help visualize where their money is. When I draw the Wealth Diamond Cash is at the Bottom Point, Tax Free is at the Top Point, Taxable is at the Left Point and Tax Deferred is at the Right Point.

The Wealth Diamond

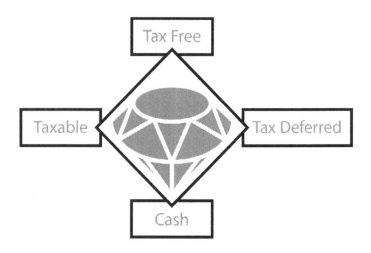

- Cash can be actual US currency, foreign currency, Certificates of Deposit, money market funds, collectibles that are readily convertible into cash such as gold coins.
- Taxable Investments are after-tax capital investments available to you.
- Tax Deferred Investments include many vehicles including IRAs, 401Ks, 403Bs, Thrift Savings Plans, Insurance products and many others.
- Tax Free Investments pretty much a Roth IRA or Roth 401K.

Logically, in which of these four basic ways would you want to make most if not all of your money? Tax Free.

Most of the guidance available about investing involves Taxable accounts. One thing I have learned is that most people have 90% of their wealth in Tax Deferred accounts. Only about 10% of people I have met have a Roth Tax Free Vehicle set up and very few of these people are taking full advantage of positioning their assets effectively in their Roth Tax Free Vehicles. There is a huge disconnect between where people should have their investments versus where they actually have their investment dollars.

As you build out your Success Plan, you need to figure out where your money is currently positioned on the Wealth Diamond. Then you need to decide where you want to position it over the next 12 months and beyond.

Living a Tax Free Life

You do not get to draw tax free income from these strategies until you are 59 1/2 but you do get to accumulate gains on a tax deferred basis until then. Your assets are basically treated the same as if they are in a tax deferred vehicle until you turn 59 1/2 when your assets and all gains on them magically become tax free.

While I understand that for many of you this can mean years and even decades before you benefit from this but let's get some perspective on how powerful this approach is. The goal is to position yourself for tax free income from 59 1/2 until you leave this earth. According to the US Social Security Administration, men who make it to the age of 60 have a life expectancy of 21.4 years and women who make it to the age of 60 have a life expectancy of 24.4 years. As this represents the average, there are many people who will live to 90, 100 and beyond.

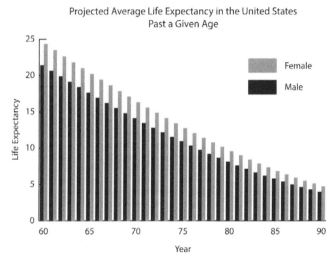

Projected Average Life Expectancy in the United States
Past a Given Age

<Source: https://www.ssa.gov/oact/STATS/table4c6.html >

These life expectancies are for Baby Boomers, many of whom live less healthy lives than the coming waves of Generation Xers and Millennials. For Generation Xers and Millennials, the life expectancy could very well be significantly longer than for the Baby Boomers due to more exercise, less smoking and eating better than previous generations.

Let's assume you started to make money in your 20's. At the age of 60 you will have generated income as an adult for 30-40 years. This tax free strategy can be designed to generate tax free income for you for 30-40 years. Basically these strategies can provide tax free income for you for 1/3 to 1/2 of your adult life assuming you are average to above average. Think of how much money you have paid or will pay in income taxes between the ages of 20 and 60. Wouldn't it be great to keep all that for yourself or for your heirs? What I am advocating here is that you keep all that money for the second half of your adult life.

Even if you are below average and you die sooner, the Tax Free Strategies that you develop for yourself can be used by your heirs so they can get the benefit of your tax free strategies when they turn 59 1/2. If your favorite T-shirt reads "I'm Spending My Kids Inheritance" than this may not be for you but most business owners I work with are interested in leaving a legacy and an impact on future generations. Not only do these strategies provide tax free income for your life, they represent one of the best estate planning vehicles available to you today.

With the current US Estate Tax system exempting over $5.4 million for individuals and $10.8 for couples, most people are not impacted by the estate tax at all. At the same time your Roth Tax Free Vehicles offer powerful tax planning tools as you can leave these to your heirs and they can benefit from the tax free assets during their lifetime. While there are a few rules that impact them including Required Minimum Distributions when they achieve 70 years old, effectively they have the ability to benefit from your powerful tax free assets.

Developing your tax free strategy may require patience if you have not already positioned your assets in a Roth Tax Free Vehicle. Jaguars hide in trees, waiting for some unsuspecting animal to walk below it. Jaguars wait for the perfect moment to pounce on their meal. This strategy takes a lot of waiting. This strategy takes a lot of patience.

In addition to the Roth Tax Free Vehicles, there have been two predominant strategies to achieve tax free results with tax deferred vehicles: Insurance or Death.

Every life insurance company and life insurance agent promotes the use of cash value policies such as whole life, universal life or whatever else they want to call them. Many of these policies offer a loan provision where the holder can take out a loan from the cash value of the policy and upon death the loan is paid back using the proceeds of the policy. Effectively, the loan was "tax free" during life and the insurance proceeds are tax free which renders this an effective tax free strategy using a tax deferred asset.

The death strategy is not beneficial for you as the person doing the dying but provides your beneficiaries with what is referred to as a Step Up in Basis which effectively gives them the appreciation of your taxable assets on a tax free basis.

Using Roth Tax Free Vehicles gives you more flexibility and upside plus you can benefit from them while you are still alive.

Doing the Math

The next sections demonstrate the benefits of making money in a Roth Tax Free vehicle both after and before you turn 59 ½. I am going through this in excruciating detail because I know the extreme resistance people have to looking at tax deferred and tax free assets as real assets that they can use for their own benefit. If you trust my math, you can skip to the conclusions of each scenario.

Tax Free Math – Static Scenario

Let's do some practical math.

Employee Math

If you generate money (M) as an employee, you pay Income Tax (IT) plus your portion of OASDI (social security and Medicare) which is 7.65%. What's leftover is your Earned Capital (C). If we assume you make $1000 and pay income tax at the blended rate of 20%, your capital yield looks like this:

EMPLOYEE MATH	STATIC
Money - Income Tax - OASDI = Earned Capital	
Money	$1000
Income Tax	-$200
OASDI	-$76.50
Earned Capital	$723.50

Self Employed Math

If you generate money (M) through self employment, you pay Income Tax (IT) plus Self Employment Tax, which is 15.3%. What's leftover is your Earned Capital (C). If we assume you make $1000 and pay income tax at the blended rate of 20%, your capital yield looks like this:

SELF-EMPLOYED MATH	STATIC
Money - Income Tax - Self-Employment Tax = Earned Capital	
Money	$1000
Income Tax	-$200
Self-Employment Tax	-$153
Earned Capital	$647

Roth Math Post 59 ½

If you generate money in a Roth Tax Free Vehicle and pull it out after turning 59 ½ you have no tax liability.

ROTH MATH POST 59 ½	STATIC
Money = Earned Capital	
Money	$1000
Earned Capital	$1000

Deferred Math Post 59 ½

If you generate money in a tax deferred vehicle and pull it out after turning 59 ½ you are responsible for income tax.

DEFERRED MATH POST 59 ½	STATIC

Money - Income Tax = Earned Capital

Money	$1000
Income Tax	$200
Earned Capital	**$800**

Roth Math Pre 59 ½

If you generate money (M) in a Roth Vehicle and pull it out prior to age 59 ½ you pay Income Tax (IT) plus an Early Withdrawal Tax, which is 10%. What's leftover is your Earned Capital (C). If we assume you make $1000 and pay income tax at the blended rate of 20%, your capital yield looks like this:

ROTH MATH PRE 59 ½	STATIC

Money - Income Tax - Early Withdrawal Tax = Earned Capital

Money	$1000
Income Tax	-$200
Early Withdrawal Tax	-$100
Earned Capital	**$700**

Deferred Math Pre 59 ½

If you generate money (M) in a Deferred Account and pull it out prior to age 59 ½ you pay Income Tax (IT) plus an Early Withdrawal Tax, which is 10%. What's left-over is your Earned Capital (C). This is the same as Roth pre-59 ½ Withdrawals. If we assume you make $1000 and pay income tax at the blended rate of 20%, your capital yield looks like this:

	STATIC
DEFERRED MATH PRE 59 ½	
Money - Income Tax - Early Withdrawal Tax = Earned Capital	
Money	$1000
Income Tax	-$200
Early Withdrawal Tax	-$100
Earned Capital	$700

Static Analysis

Here is a summary of results:

1.	Roth Post 59 ½	$1000
2.	Tax Deferred Post 59 ½	$800
3.	Employee	$723.50
4.	Roth Pre 59 ½	$700
5.	Tax Deferred Pre 59 ½	$700
6.	Self Employed Business Owner	$647

In a static earning example both the post 59 ½ earning scenarios represent the best outcome, with working as an employee being 3rd, earning in a Roth or Tax Deferred Vehicle tied for 4th and earning as a self employed business owner as 6th or last.

Tax Free Dynamic Scenario

Normally the self employed business owner will be able to earn a premium to overcome the tax benefits of employees and cover other associated business expenses. This premium would also apply to any Roth Tax Free Vehicle Strategies or Tax Deferred Vehicle Strategies. If you could not make more money, why would you own a business? This scenario assumes every Active Investor Opportunity generates more income than being an employee. I use a 20% bump ($1200) but certainly you can make more.

Employee Math – Same as Static Example

If you generate money (M) as an employee, you pay Income Tax (IT) plus your portion of OASDI (social security and Medicare) which is 7.65%. What's leftover is your Earned Capital (C). If we assume you make $1000 and pay income tax at the blended rate of 20%, your capital yield looks like this:

```
                                              DYNAMIC
                      EMPLOYEE MATH

         Money - Income Tax - OASDI = Earned Capital

         Money                        $1000
         Income Tax                   -$200
         OASDI                        -$76.50
         ─────────────────────────────────────
         Earned Capital               $723.50
```

Self Employed Math

If you generate money (M) through self employment,
you pay Income Tax (IT) plus Self Employment Tax,
which is 15.3%. What's leftover is your Earned Capital
(C). If we assume you make $1200 and pay income tax
at the blended rate of 20%, your capital yield looks like
this:

```
                                              DYNAMIC
                    SELF-EMPLOYED MATH

   Money - Income Tax - Self-Employment Tax = Earned Capital

         Money                        $1200
         Income Tax                   -$240
         Self-Employment Tax          -$183.60
         ─────────────────────────────────────
         Earned Capital               $776.40
```

CHRIS KOOMEY

Roth Math Post 59 ½

If you generate money in a Roth Tax Free Vehicle and pull it out after turning 59 ½ you have no tax liability.

ROTH MATH POST 59 ½	DYNAMIC
Money = Earned Capital	
Money	$1200
Earned Capital	$1200

Deferred Math Post 59 ½

If you generate money in a tax deferred vehicle and pull it out after turning 59 ½ you are responsible for income tax.

DEFERRED MATH POST 59 ½	DYNAMIC
Money - Income Tax = Earned Capital	
Money	$1200
Income Tax	$240
Earned Capital	$960

Roth Math Pre 59 ½

If you generate money (M) in a Roth Vehicle and pull it out prior to age 59 ½ you pay Income Tax (IT) plus an Early Withdrawal Tax, which is 10%. What's leftover is your Earned Capital (C). If we assume you make $1200 and pay income tax at the blended rate of 20%, your capital yield looks like this:

ROTH MATH PRE 59 ½	DYNAMIC
Money - Income Tax - Early Withdrawal Tax = Earned Capital	
Money	$1200
Income Tax	-$240
Early Withdrawal Tax	-$120
Earned Capital	$840

Deferred Math Pre 59 ½

If you generate money (M) in a Deferred Account and pull it out prior to age 59 ½ you pay Income Tax (IT) plus an Early Withdrawal Tax, which is 10%. What's leftover is your Earned Capital (C). This is the same as Roth pre-59 ½ Withdrawals. If we assume you make $1200 and pay income tax at the blended rate of 20%, your capital yield looks like this:

DYNAMIC

DEFERRED MATH PRE 59 ½

Money - Income Tax - Early Withdrawal Tax = Earned Capital

Money	$1200
Income Tax	-$240
Early Withdrawal Tax	-$120
Earned Capital	$840

Dynamic Analysis

Here is a summary of results:

1. Roth Post 59 ½ $1200
2. Tax Deferred Post 59 ½ $960
3. Roth Pre 59 ½ $840
4. Tax Deferred Pre 59 ½ $840
5. Self Employed Business Owner $776.40
6. Employee $723.50

Taxed Earnings   Tax-Free Earnings

In this scenario, the post 59 ½ strategies hold their positions as best and second best, while the under 59 ½ scenarios tie for 3d, self employed business owner 4th and employee 5th.

Through these mathematical exercises I am certainly not trying to discourage you from business ownership or self employment (although employment is another issue). I am however hoping to demonstrate to you that developing opportunities as an Active Investor in Roth Tax Free Vehicles and Tax Deferred Vehicles are a rational part of any Active Investor overall success plan. Math doesn't lie.

You are certainly happy to be a business owner. Why not use these skills to generate better returns as an Active Investor using Roth Tax Free Vehicles? People still work as an Employee even though they are taxed in the highest tax circumstance. Employees that lose their job in their 50s often can not receive the salary they are accustomed to which is why Active Investing is something they need to explore. I realize the financial services industry has conditioned you to fear pulling money from your tax free and tax deferred accounts. Simple math shows that using Roth Tax Free Vehicles as an Active Investor will yield better net after tax returns for you than running a business and most likely as an employee.

There are restrictions in using the Roth Tax Free Vehicles and Tax Deferred Vehicles that make them unwieldy or inefficient as your primary stream of income but allow them to be appropriate for your secondary or tertiary income and wealth strategies so you can prepare to unleash your financial power.

CHAPTER 3

AVOIDING THINGS THAT START WITH "I"

My friend Doug used to advise that you generally want to avoid things that start with the letter "I" as in Incurable, Insane and Indictment. When it comes to tax free strategies you also want to avoid "International." There are numerous tax havens around the world many of which claim to provide you tax free or tax preferred treatment of your investments. Unfortunately, your Uncle Sam does not see things the same way.

As they have increased the requirements around declaring international assets for US citizens your tax free international tax haven may not be so tax free after all. In this age of money tracking you will not be able to hide your assets so you are better off not trying. As a

US citizen you are required to pay income tax on your worldwide income. Unless you are willing to renounce your citizenship, the international tax haven route is not as attractive as it might sound.

In the past, the primary thing that international tax havens provided was secrecy. While that is still a purported benefit, the US has actively been obtaining access to information from these tax havens in the name of anti-terrorism. The reality is that tax havens have lost their ability to deliver on their promise of secrecy.

The Panama Papers, which printed the names of many politicians and others who were trying to rely on the "secrecy" of international tax havens, demonstrate that in the 21st century there are no more secrets. They may not be publicly known, but eventually if you are trying to do something you are not supposed to be doing, your secret will be swept into public view. The lesson is to stop trying to get away with something and just figure out where is the best place to position your income without doing something illegal. (Another "I" word).

Beyond long lost relatives, abandoned bank accounts, new found treasures and other fantasies, there are many perils related to international investing. International opportunities are ripe for financial confidence games such as Ponzi schemes and the like. Alan Stanford conducted a multi-billion dollar Ponzi scheme using the construct of an international bank. What finally did him in was not that the Ponzi scheme crumbled but that he inexplicably opened branches in the US and subjected himself to the jurisdiction of the US government.

<Source: Dallas Morning News>

Stanford's Ponzi scheme started in the 1980's and existed until 2009. He started in Montserrat and then eventually moved to Antigua. His premise was simple: guarantee above average interest rates on "safe" investments. Stanford's bank marketed CDs at 6% interest and money flowed in. Stanford famously said it was amazing what people would do for a couple of extra points of interest.

But the people weren't just any people. Most of the people that were sending him money were not the widows and orphans targeted by traditional Ponzi schemes. Stanford was able to keep his Ponzi scheme going because much of the money he collected came from people who were trying to evade taxes or tracking in their home country. Some were government officials siphoning money from their government. Some were drug dealers who were making so much money they needed somewhere "safe" to put their money. I am sure there were some enterprising US oil men who were trying to shield their money from US taxes as well.

If your clients are in jail or dead, you don't need to return their money, which allowed the money to keep on flowing. What did him in was as Central and South American countries became less corrupt, he decided to move to the US as a source of more money flow. By exposing himself to US regulators, he exposed his

Ponzi scheme to a government that was not as willing to look the other way. Stanford had collected over $8 billion dollars in deposits but less than a billion could be liquidated when the scheme came tumbling down.

One of the lessons is that if you are scamming people that are evading the law, they are less likely to require you to prove you are on the up and up. If you are evading the law you are more susceptible to schemes and scams. This is one of the keys to a good confidence game. Get the mark to cross a line and they are less likely to question the con when they are taken advantage of.

I am not against international investments. In fact, I think there are great ways to protect yourself from the depreciation of the US dollar by investing in international real estate, businesses and currency. The key to their success is your active involvement. Entering investments for their purported tax free benefits is likely not going to give you the results you desire and may entail a lot more risk than you planned for.

The right way to plan not to pay taxes is to follow the rules that your government lays out for you. There are legal ways to not pay taxes so you don't have to outsmart anyone. Don't try to be too smart. Just follow the yellow brick road.

Island of Enchantment

Puerto Rico is known as the Island of Enchantment and even though "Island" starts with an "I", it may be the most enchanting legal way to reduce or eliminate your tax bill. Puerto Rico is a territory of the United States that provides it with many benefits by being in the US sphere of influence without being subject to US income taxes. Puerto Rico is still subject to other US taxes like Social Security.

Greetings

PUERTO RICO

Six Tax Free or Tax Reduction Strategies

1. Establish an export services company
2. Become a bona fide resident
3. Move a financial management or investment company
4. Establish an investment fund
5. Pursue tourism development projects
6. Operate insurance and re-insurance operations in Puerto Rico

Now before 2012 this was not such a great deal because you were still subject to Puerto Rican income taxes, which were comparable to or higher than the US, tax rates. However in 2012, with an eye towards attracting service based businesses, the Puerto Rican government greatly reduced the tax rates for dividend and interest income as well as for service based businesses. The tax rate for qualified dividends and interest is ZERO. Capital gains earned while a resident of Puerto Rico are also tax free. Long term capital gains earned prior to becoming a resident of Puerto Rico are taxed at 5 %. The tax rate for service businesses is 4%. This allows US citizens to live in Puerto Rico and enjoy the benefits of a low or no tax regime. The key is you need to be a bona fide resident of Puerto Rico.

These tax benefits are available to people who have not been residents of Puerto Rico for the 6 years previous.

If you are a U.S. citizen or resident alien, you will satisfy the presence test for the entire tax year if you meet ONE of the following conditions:

1. You were present in the relevant possession for at least 183 days during the tax year.
2. You were present in the relevant possession for at least 549 days during the 3-year period that includes the current tax year and the 2 immediately preceding tax years. During each year of the

3-year period, you must be present in the relevant possession for at least 60 days.

3. You were present in the United States for no more than 90 days during the tax year.

4. You had earned income in the United States of no more than a total of $3,000 and were present for more days in the relevant possession than in the United States during the tax year. Earned income is pay for personal services performed, such as wages, salaries, or professional fees.

5. You had no significant connection to the United States during the tax year.

See IRS publication for more information: https://www.irs.gov/publications/p570/ch01.html

Americans don't have to renounce their citizenship or pay an exit tax of 23.8% on unrealized capital gains when they move to Puerto Rico. While the US taxes its citizens on their worldwide income, Section 933 of the U.S. Tax Code exempts Puerto Rico sourced income from federal income tax.

If you are a bona fide resident of Puerto Rico during the entire tax year, you generally are not required to file a U.S. federal income tax return if your only income is from sources within Puerto Rico. However, if you also have income from sources outside of Puerto Rico, including from U.S. sources, you are required to file a U.S. federal income tax return if such amount is above the U.S. filing threshold. Nevertheless, a bona fide resident of Puerto Rico with a U.S. filing obligation, generally will not report Puerto Rican source income on a U.S. income tax return.

If It's (Tax) Free, It's For Me

In 2012, Puerto Rico changed its tax code to turn itself into a tax haven for U.S. citizens that become residents of Puerto Rico. Act 20, the Export Services Act, and Act 22, the Individual Investors Act, reduces or eliminates most federal income taxes on interest, dividends and capital gains and provide for a low income tax rate for Puerto Rico based service businesses. This provides a great incentive to develop Puerto Rico sourced income as well as to derive income from interest, dividends and capital gains if you are willing to live in Puerto Rico for at least half the year.

Mechanics of Act 20 and 22

In order to benefit from Act 20 and 22, you must submit an online application through the Department of Economic Development & Commerce (DDEC) for Act

20 and through the Office of Industrial Tax Exemption of Puerto Rico for Act 22. Effectively you will create a contract between the Government of Puerto Rico and you. Tax benefits will be secured during the term of the agreement, regardless of changes in the Puerto Rico tax laws afterwards. The agreements have a term of 20 years with possible extensions beyond that term.

The Export Services Act (Act 20) promotes the development of service based businesses in Puerto Rico with the goal of providing services globally. In order to qualify, businesses cannot have any previous connections, dealings or nexus with Puerto Rico.

Qualifying businesses under Act 20 pay a fixed income tax rate of 4% (3% in case of strategic services) and are exempt from 90% of personal and real property taxes for the first 5 years of operation. Additionally qualifying businesses receive reduced tax rates for municipal taxes. For owners of qualifying businesses, distribution of earnings and profits are tax free.

The Individual Investors Act (Act 22) attracts individual investors to Puerto Rico by providing a total exemption from local income taxes on all passive income (dividends, interest & capital gains) from the point they become legal bona fide Puerto Rican residents. In order to benefit from Act 22, you must buy a residence in Puerto Rico within two years.

Bonus Tax Savings

The International Financial Center Regulatory Act (Act 273) provides similar incentives to locate financial businesses in Puerto Rico. Qualifying entities must be formed outside of Puerto Rico and employ four people in Puerto Rico.

Qualifying entities must have paid in capital of at least $5 million and when approved will receive a 15 year agreement that caps their company income tax at 4% and provides a 6% income tax for dividends and other distribution of profits. Qualifying entities receive a full exemption from personal, real and municipal property taxes.

The Private Equity Funds Act (Act 185) improves access to capital for entrepreneurs and businesses. The Act provides a structure for investors to deploy capital with limited personal liability and without double taxation, while enjoying certain tax benefits such as exemptions, deductions and fixed income tax rates. Qualifying funds are "Private Equity Funds" and "Puerto Rico Private Equity Funds" and must have $10 million paid in capital within two years of formation. 80% of investments are to be made in non-public securities. Qualifying companies can be formed in Puerto Rico, US or a foreign jurisdiction.

Qualifying funds are exempt from taxation in interest, dividends and capital gains. Qualifying funds are exempt form personal, real and municipal taxes as well. Accredited investors pay 10% income tax on interest and dividend from the fund and 0% on capital gains realized through the fund. Capital gains from selling their interest in the fund are subject to a 5% tax. General partners, registered investment advisors and private equity firms pay 5% income tax on interest and dividends.

The Tourism Development Act (Act 74) facilitates tourism initiatives. Benefits are in effect for 10 years from opening of the project with a possible 10-year extension under the Act. Qualifying projects can receive tax credits and exemptions from income tax and personal, real and municipal taxes.

The International Insurance Center (Act 98) provides a competitive environment for international insurers and reinsurers to cover risks outside of Puerto Rico with attractive tax benefits. Basically this allows Puerto Rico to provide access to the US market to programs that have been primarily located in former tax havens.

The Last US Tax Haven

Puerto Rico is taking advantage of the U.S. crackdown on offshore tax havens. By providing similar services as previous tax havens and outstanding tax treatment for individuals and companies to relocate to Puerto Rico, Puerto Rico has positioned itself as the last true tax haven for US citizens (other than Roth Tax Free Vehicles).

Six Tax Free or Tax Reduction Strategies offered by Puerto Rico are:

1. Establish an Export Services Company;
2. Become a bona fide resident and reduce or eliminate taxes on dividends, interest and capital gains;
3. Move a financial management or investment company;
4. Establish an Investment Fund;
5. Pursue Tourism Development Projects; and
6. Operate insurance and re-insurance operations in Puerto Rico

Puerto Rico offers sun, sand and surf while you plan to not pay taxes. If you want to stay closer to home, your Roth Tax Free Vehicles provide you with great opportunities as well.

CHAPTER 4

TAX FREE BUSINESS OPPORTUNITIES

I n order to break free from the Financial Services Passive Investment Model you need to identify businesses that have the potential to generate more significant returns as an Active Investor. Here are the rules to fund your Roth Tax Free Vehicle Business that you will use as an Active Investor.

1. The Company must be newly formed
2. The only initial shareholder of the company can be the Roth Tax Free Vehicle
3. You can not receive payment or benefit (direct, indirect or otherwise) for services rendered.
4. You can serve as an uncompensated member of the Board of Directors

5. Your immediate family members can not receive payment or benefits (direct, indirect or otherwise) from the company

6. In order to make this work, you will need another source of income from another business or from your assets until you are 59 1/2

You ask "Why on earth would I want to set up a company where I can't be paid?" The two benefits of this approach provide you with tax free income post 59 ½ plus a powerful estate planning tool for you and your heirs.

Benefit 1: The Roth Tax Free Vehicle can accumulate tax free dividends as the owner of the company

Benefit 2: The Roth Tax Free Vehicle can distribute tax free dividends as the owner of the company once you achieve 59 ½

Benefit 3: The Roth Tax Free Vehicle can be inherited by your heirs and provide them with tax free income when they are 59 ½

The Code that establishes IRAs (26 USC 408) and Roth IRAs (26 USC 408A) provides the structure for doing this, but the key case that makes this clear is

Swanson v Commissioner 106 T.C. 76. https://scholar. google.com/scholar_case?case=152779634169262791 30&hl=en&as_sdt=6&as_vis=1&oi=scholarr

In this case, Swanson funded an IRA and that IRA purchased original issue stock in a Company. At some later date, Swanson became the sole director of the Company. The Company generated profits and distributed profits as dividends to the IRA.

26 USC 4975 provides for "Tax on Prohibited Transactions" and in part defines Prohibited Transactions as including any act by a disqualified person whereby he "deals with the income or assets of a plan in his own interest or for his own account." Prior to issuing shares to

the IRA, the Company had no shares or shareholders so it could not fit into the definition of a disqualified person at the time of the original transaction. Once shares are issued and the Company is operational you and your relatives can not receive direct economic benefit from the Company except through dividends because then you and the IRA would be disqualified persons.

I just laid out the straightforward rules but I know you are already thinking of ways to try to game the opportunity. I advise you to stop trying to game the opportunity and accept it for what it is - an incredibly powerful strategy for you to obtain tax free income when you are 59 ½ and over as a component of your overall success plan.

Remember - Avoid things that start with an "I". Are there risks with this strategy? Yes. If you lose capital, your capital is gone with no corresponding tax offset. This is why you want to consider low risk cash flow businesses.

Another consideration is that your chosen business may only be effective for a certain amount of time:

1. With your accumulated tax free profits you may want to plan to fund additional cash flow businesses

2. You may want to plan to sell your cash flow business at some point and roll your proceeds into another Tax Free Business Opportunity

These two approaches allow you to maintain the effectiveness of this strategy throughout the second half of your adult life.

Cash Flow Business

Proven business models that can be staffed without you are the best candidates for a cash flow business using your Roth Tax Free Vehicles. An established franchise business can provide you with the structure and the longevity that would make this worthwhile.

Because of your inability to capture or recapture losses, you do not want to establish a startup or an untested business model in this strategy. Many franchises represent untested business models so don't just blindly put a franchise into the cash flow business model. You want a business you can hire a manager for that does not need much more than basic oversight on your part. Additionally this manager can not be part of your immediate family. Businesses that may fit this model are convenience stores, cleaning services, food prep businesses or a business model that you have successfully run yourself.

Angel Investing

Angel Investing through Roth Tax Free Vehicles is a boom or bust proposition. Angel Investing by its nature is high risk, high reward and is not for everyone. You don't get to offset your losses. You may not get paid for a while, if ever.

The risks inherent in Angel Investing are:

1. Finding an investable business model
2. Finding trustworthy implementers of an investable business model
3. Finding competent implementers of an investable business model
4. Achieving compensation for your investment in a reasonable amount of time

If you do a good job of minimizing these risks you still have the basic probabilities that if you do a good job:

- 1 out of 5 will succeed
- 2 out of 5 will muddle long and will eventually fail to achieve their potential but may return some of your capital
- 2 out of 5 will fail spectacularly

So Angel Investing is not for the faint of heart but there are also great potential rewards involved with it. Angel Investing can be a way to keep yourself engaged after you have reduced your role in your primary business.

Royalties - IP Development and Licensing

Often in the development of an IT company, the most valuable part of the company is not the cash flow but the intellectual property that powers the business model. Often the ownership of intellectual property is placed in a holding company that collects royalties from the company using the patents. This Intellectual property can also be licensed to other companies. As royalties can represent a significant cash flow that is not based on your efforts and is a great application for your Roth Tax Free Entity to build wealth tax free for you.

This is also a great application for creators of books, movies, songs and other valuable content that has commercial value. Use your Roth Tax Free Vehicle to hold the IP and collect royalties on it.

Real Estate

Generally Real Estate Investing is best executed in taxable accounts due to the generous tax code provisions that encourage real estate opportunities. However, one popular strategy that is not treated well in taxable accounts is rehabbing which is popularly known as flipping. For house flippers, the tax code requires a chunk of profits on every deal, which reduces profits but more realistically gets house flippers in tax trouble because they don't realize they are actually holding money for the benefit of their Uncle Sam. Because house flippers treat this as their own, they can neglect to pay taxes, which can drag down their business. This issue can be eliminated by using Roth Tax Free Vehicles to fund your house flipping strategy.

Purchasing tax liens is another real estate strategy that can be used effectively in a Roth Tax Free Vehicle. Localities sell tax liens on properties that have not paid back taxes as a means of accelerating their collection of tax money. Tax liens can provide a consistent income from interest plus upside in the event that the property is foreclosed upon.

The negative of using Roth Tax Free Vehicles for these transactions is you might find it more difficult to finance your transactions so you lose the benefit of leverage that helps most real estate transactions.

If you can self fund your real estate investing account, you can realize the full benefit of the profit of your transaction. The Roth Tax Free Vehicle allow you to build up assets which can be used to generate tax free income when you get to 59 ½.

If you are able to build up a significant amount of assets in a Roth IRA you can use the entity to own the properties and provide you with tax free rental income. Generally you are better off doing this in a taxable structure but in some circumstances it might make sense.

Financial Trading

The easiest business for utilizing Roth Tax Free vehicles is trading financial assets. There are numerous companies that allow you to trade stocks, options, futures and FOREX (currencies) in Roth Tax Free Vehicles. Plus you don't have to worry about the restrictions for your involvement as you do with the other business structures.

In order to trade successfully, you should get educated and use an established system. One of the businesses that I am involved with, the Online Trading Academy provides an extensive education program available in major metropolitan areas in the United States as well as in several locations worldwide. Online Trading Academy education provides lifetime access to in person and online education that includes live trading labs and a lot of personalized attention.

Roth Tax Free Vehicle Strategies

In this chapter I have provided you with 5 strategic ways for you to use your Roth Tax Free Vehicles to generate tax free income and build wealth.

1. Cash Flow Businesses
2. Angel Investing
3. Intellectual Property Holding
4. Real Estate
5. Financial Trading

Within each of these strategies, there are countless ways for you to build the tax free income strategies that fit your overall success plan.

CHAPTER 5

MECHANICS AND FUNDING STRATEGIES

Y ou can certainly start a funding strategy as early as possible but the reality is most people wait. There are two basic ways to get assets into a Roth Tax Free vehicle: Conversion and Contribution.

Conversion

Conversion currently has no limits or income restrictions on it. Basically for people under 59 ½, you can convert any amount you hold in a traditional IRA or tax deferred vehicle such as a 401K from a previous employer. People over 59 ½ can not only convert any amount held in traditional IRAs or tax deferred vehicles from previous employers but can also generally transfer tax deferred funds from their current employer.

The reason the rules for conversion are so wide open is that every dollar you convert is subject to income tax less any basis that you may have in the funds. But remember taxes are just a cost of doing business. You are effectively paying those taxes to create tax free assets. Better to pay the taxes than paying an attorney to create some fancy strategy for you.

Another key point with this tax payment is while you transfer tax deferred assets, you can pay the tax from taxable assets. This effectively allows you to convert taxable assets into tax free assets. This is an incredibly powerful opportunity that is incredibly underutilized.

Contribution

Contribution wise there are limits but if you plan ahead you can position significant assets in Roth Tax Free Vehicles. I am going to use a 50 year old as an example because special rules apply once you turn 50. Plus I just turned 50 so this shows there is more to turning 50 than qualifying for AARP.

The basic maximum contribution rate for a Roth IRA is $5500. If you are over 50 you can contribute an extra $1000, which means you can contribute $6500 per year.

Direct contributions to a Roth IRA have income limitations, which begin at $117,000 for individuals and $184,000 for people filing jointly in 2016. If you earn over $133,000 as an individual or $194,000 for people filing jointly you can not contribute directly to a Roth IRA.

However, everyone can contribute to a traditional IRA in the same amounts $5500 for those under 50 and $6500 over 50 with deductibility impacted by the same income limits above. Let's assume you make more than the $133,000 or $194,000 income limit for deductibility. This means you will have a basis equal to the full amount of your contribution.

At some later date you can convert this traditional IRA into a Roth IRA. You pay taxes on the amount that you move minus your basis. If you contribute $6500 then you subtract your basis of $6500 you have no taxable income on this amount when you convert it. You only have taxes if you earn money on your contribution, which you would owe in a taxable account anyway.

The best way to contribute to a Roth TAX free vehicle is to use a Roth 401K. More than half of 401Ks include a Roth provision. Even if your 401K does not include a Roth 401K provision, you can ask your human resource professional to add it and it should have a minimal cost impact on your company. There are no income limitations on contributing to a Roth 401K.

If you are a business owner you have control to set up the 401K with a Roth Provision. If you own a company where you are the sole worker you can set up a solo 401K, which allows you the most flexibility in making contributions.

Everyone can contribute up to the amount of earned income or $18,000 whichever is less. For those of us over 50, we can contribute an additional $6000 per year.

Additionally, with proper profit sharing or SEP plans an additional $35,000 can be contributed into tax deferred accounts per year per individual. You can choose to convert this when you turn 59 ½.

Each year everyone can contribute $23,500 into Roth Tax free vehicles and an additional $35,000 into tax deferred vehicles. If you are over 50, you can contribute $30,500 into Roth Tax Free Vehicles.

Funding Strategy for a 30 Year Old

For 30 Year olds, I am providing 8 scenarios to implement your tax free business strategy. Four of these strategies assume you contribute for 10 years and 4 scenarios assume you contribute for 30 years. I realize that doing anything consistently for 30 years is extremely unlikely and doesn't account for possible changes in contribution rules over this time. However, this is the standard approach used by the financial services industry and shows you the power and potential of fully committing to these strategies.

I am assuming you achieve either 3% or 6% in each scenario. 3% is a reasonable return to expect with long term bonds. 6% is a reasonable rate of return to expect with 60-40 split or 50-50 split between a stock index and a long term bond index. I realize that life and investing is not a straight line proposition but these are fairly benign projected returns. Your results will vary but these provide decent ballpark estimates.

The first two scenarios assume you dedicate your full annual IRA contribution to your tax free strategy for 30 years. The math uses $5500 for 20 years and $6500 for 10 years. Scenario 1 assumes a 3% straight line return and scenario 2 assumes a 6% straight line return. In Scenario 1 at the age of 60 you would have above $280,000. In Scenario 2 you would have around $480,000.

Roth Free Tax Vehicles (RFTV) Funding Scenarios 1-4
Beginning at Age 30

1. Maximum Contribution, 6% Return
2. Maximum Contribution, 3% Return
3. Minimum Contribution, 6% Return
4. Minimum Contribution, 3% Return

Age (Years)

Millions of Dollars

In Scenarios 3 and 4, I assume you totally max out your contributions to a Roth IRA and a Roth 401K for 30 years. In Scenario 3, with a straight line return of 3% you would have over $1.2 million. In Scenario 4 with a projected straight line return of 6% you would have over $2 million. I realize that conventional financial services tells you if you use their strategies you need at least these amounts. With the tax free strategies I have identified herein, these amounts are probably overkill but great if you achieve them. I also realize some of you are fanatics and want to be all in so I don't want to put a damper on your enthusiasm.

In Scenarios 5 and 6 I assume you contribute your maximum IRA contribution for 10 years between the ages of 30 and 40. In Scenario 5 with a straight line return of 3% you would achieve over $110,000 for your tax free strategies. In Scenario 6 with a straight line return of 6% you would achieve over $240,000 for your tax free strategies.

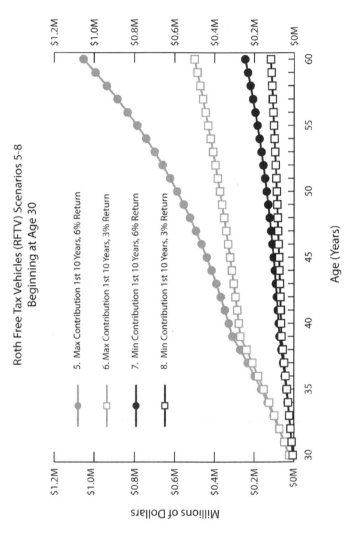

Roth Free Tax Vehicles (RFTV) Scenarios 5-8
Beginning at Age 30

5. Max Contribution 1st 10 Years, 6% Return
6. Max Contribution 1st 10 Years, 3% Return
7. Min Contribution 1st 10 Years, 6% Return
8. Min Contribution 1st 10 Years, 3% Return

Age (Years)

Millions of Dollars

In Scenarios 7 and 8, I assume you dedicate your maximum IRA Contribution and Roth 401K Contribution for a period of 10 years between the ages of 30 and 40. In Scenario 7 with a 3% straight line return you would achieve over $500,000. In Scenario 8 with a 6% straight line return you would achieve over $1 million to dedicate to your tax free strategies.

Funding Strategy for a 40 Year Old

Scenarios 9 through 16 follow the same basic structure as scenarios 1 through 8 but assume you start your contributions at age 40.

Scenarios 9 and 10 assume you dedicate your full IRA contribution from the age of 40 through 60 to fund your tax free strategies. Scenario 9 assumes a straight line 3% return and results in just short of $150,000 available to your tax free strategies. Scenario 10 assumes a straight line 6% return and results in over $200,000 available to fund your tax free strategies.

Roth Free Tax Vehicles (RFTV) Funding Scenarios 9-12
Beginning at Age 40

9. Maximum Contribution, 6% Return
10. Maximum Contribution, 3% Return
11. Minimum Contribution, 6% Return
12. Minimum Contribution, 3% Return

Millions of Dollars

Age (Years)

Scenarios 11 and 12 assumes you dedicate your full IRA contribution and Roth 401K contribution from the age of 40 to 60 to fund your tax free strategies. Scenario 11 assumes a straight line 3% return and yields over $700,000 for your tax free strategies. Scenario 12 assumes a straight line 6% return and yields over $950,000.

Scenarios 13 and 14 assume you dedicate your full IRA Contribution for 10 years between the ages of 40 and 50. Scenario 13 assumes a 3% straight line return and yields over $85,000 for your tax free strategies. Scenario 14 assumes a 6% straight line return and yields over $135,000 for your tax free strategies.

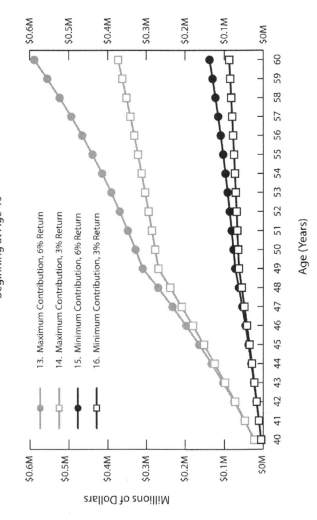

Roth Free Tax Vehicles (RFTV) Funding Scenarios 13-16
Beginning at Age 40

13. Maximum Contribution, 6% Return
14. Maximum Contribution, 3% Return
15. Minimum Contribution, 6% Return
16. Minimum Contribution, 3% Return

Millions of Dollars

Age (Years)

Scenarios 15 and 16 assume you dedicate your maximum IRA contribution and Roth 401K contribution for 10 years between the ages of 40 and 50. Scenario 15 assumes a 3% straight line return and yields over $360,000 to dedicate to your tax free strategies at the age of 60. Scenario 16 assumes a 6% straight line return and yields over $550,000 available to fund your tax free strategies.

Funding Strategy for a 50 Year Old

As a 50 year old, you are probably in the best position to maximize this strategy so I am not going to give you the opportunity to contribute on the low end of the spectrum because at this stage you should be all in. Let's assume you dedicate your full IRA and Roth 401K contributions plus your additional tax deferred strategies over ten years and maximize your contributions. You will have contributed $305,000 into Roth Tax Free Vehicles and $350,000 into tax deferred vehicles. If you convert the $350,000 from tax deferred into a Roth Tax Free Vehicle you will owe $100,000 to $150,000 in taxes. If you pull the money from the tax deferred account you will have over $500,000 available to you in Roth Tax Free Vehicles. If you use taxable money to pay your taxes you will have at least $650,000 in Roth Tax Free Vehicles. This amount can be greater if you get any kind of positive return on your money over the decade you have been building up this asset.

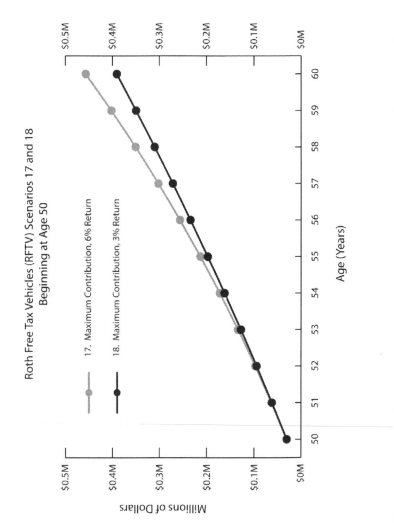

Roth Free Tax Vehicles (RFTV) Scenarios 17 and 18
Beginning at Age 50

17. Maximum Contribution, 6% Return

18. Maximum Contribution, 3% Return

Age (Years)

Millions of Dollars

For 50 year olds I have run two scenarios related to maximizing your IRA and Roth 401K contributions. Scenario 17 assumes a 3% straight line return and yields about $390,000 for your tax free strategies. Scenario 18 assumes a 6% return and yields over $450,000 to dedicate to your tax free strategies.

Pouncing on Your Tax Free Business Opportunities

Now that you have significant dollars in your Roth Tax Free account, you can implement one, two or three of the strategies we identified in Chapter 4. You can establish a significant cash flow business. You can fund a significant number of Angel Investments. You can build some real Intellectual Property. You can do some significant house flipping. You can generate significant income with financial assets.

Importantly, you have positioned yourself to not pay taxes for the rest of your life, which for many of you may be 30 or 40 years. The benefits you can derive from these active investor strategies are significantly more than what you can derive from passive conventional financial services strategies. And a lot more fun.

Mechanics of Setting Up

The problem with most Roth Tax Free Vehicles is that they are set up by passive financial investment companies so they are only able to hold passive financial investments. The IRS rules allow you to hold a broader range of assets.

There are several providers who can develop customized plans to allow you to hold a broad range of assets. If you are the sole owner of a company you can set up a Solo 401K. The same providers who set up Solo 401Ks can also help you develop customized plan for you and your business. The cost to set these up may be minimal or range into the several thousand dollars depending on their complexity.

Here are a few to choose from but you can search the web for more if you like:

OTA Tax Pros:
http://www.otataxpros.com/contact/contact.aspx
Or call Michael Atias Toll Free (U.S.): 855-OTA-PROS (855-682-7767)
Email: **info@otataxpros.com**

My Solo 401K Financial:
https://www.mysolo401k.net/about-my-solo-401k-financial/

Solo 401K:
http://www.solo401k.com/

Leaving a Tax Free Legacy

Over and above providing you with tax free income and the ability to build significant and sustainable businesses to fund the second half of your adult life, the ability to leave a tax free legacy to your heirs is probably the most powerful and impactful benefit of pursuing the tax free business strategies included in this book.

This does not require any complex trust or estate documents. You simply need to identify them as beneficiaries and your tax free vehicles will pass to them on your death.

Living a Tax Free Life

In <u>Plan to Not Pay Taxes</u>, I have provided you with an understanding of the importance of Active Investing and how to incorporate tax free strategies into your overall Success Plan. Puerto Rico as the Last US Tax Haven may be an attractive option for many of you who like waves, sand and sun. Roth Tax Free Vehicles provide opportunities for you to generate tax free income for the rest of your life in the US.

Now you just need to get started.

Bonus Retirement Guide
For Business Owners

We all need someone to provide us guidance at times whether it's a mentor, a parent, an attorney or just someone who has walked in our shoes before. The Business Godfather is designed to pull together collective wisdom for each of us as we build businesses and manage our own personal financial affairs in the turbulent 21st century.

For us to build our own world, we need to think about ourselves, our businesses and our finances outside the conventional approaches that are holding us back. Guide to Retirement Options for Business Owners throws away conventional approaches to retirement and will get you to start making business-like decisions related to your own Personal Financial Business so you can retire when and in the manner you want.

My goal is to remove the fear and misunderstanding related to retirement options for business owners so you can reap the rewards that you have worked so hard for yourself, your family and your legacy. The options that I highlight are available to you through conventional brokers and can be put into action with between 30 minutes to 4 hours per month depending on the number of approaches you put into effect for your Personal Financial Business. As with all trades of time for money, we can be a victim or get on the right side of the trade – I want you on the right side of the trade.

This Guide will not explore every nuance or detail of the strategies I present and is intended to raise your awareness that you have better options available to you than those presented by the Financial Fee Extraction Industry.

The question for you is "How important is it for you to retire the way you want?"

I know your gut answer is "Very Important" - however, your actions tell a different story. How you spend your time demonstrates your priorities in life. The reality is that most people don't care enough to spend much of any time on their retirement. They want to put their money in an account and magically wake up 40 years later with a big chunk of money. And why is that what you expect? Well, the first page of every investment book starts with the same basic premise, "if you put your money in the S&P 500 and wait 40 years you will get a big chunk of money."

Every Personal Finance website includes retirement calculators and all sorts of ways to project that if you could just get a consistent rate of return over a period of years, you will be able to retire the way you want. Read a Mutual Fund Prospectus and they will show you a straight line projection of what you would receive if you got a consistent rate of return over a period of years.

Every aspiring entrepreneur has made the graph showing a graceful curve of consistent growth by which they will conquer their industry. Just like in these aspirational businesses, your personal finance results rarely follow a straight line.

I am going to refer to your Personal Financial Business so often in this Guide that I am going to capitalize it at every turn. We have been trained to think that a different set of rules applies to our personal finances than we would apply to run our real businesses whether as an employee, consultant or business owner. The conventional personal finance approaches provide some good general principles but have been co-opted by the retail financial services industry (the Financial Fee Extraction Industry as I refer to it) to such an extent to push people into their favorite high fee products ranging from mutual funds, to lifecycle funds, to annuities and many other products not designed to help you retire but to use your assets as a source of fees. The Financial Fee Extraction Industry is not compensated by performance but in how well they aggregate assets. This asset aggregation model has allowed your financial goals to be subjugated to the goals of your financial advisor.

Pre-1980's very few individuals owned stocks and the financial services industry was able to make money through high commissions and by pocketing the spread between willing buyers and willing sellers. Most individuals had no interest in the stock market. In the early 1980's, Individual Retirement Accounts (IRAs) and 401ks were authorized and created the Financial Fee Extraction Industry of today focused on mutual funds and annuities.

Nervous About Retirement? – You Should Be

Or at least the conventional personal financial press and Financial Fee Extraction Industry want you to be nervous. In a seemingly continuous rotation we see the same sorts of articles pop up with headlines like:

"Insolvency looms for federal entitlement programs, government warns"
By Noam N. Levey, L.A. Times, May 13, 2011

"Study: Half of Those Nearing Retirement May Run Out of Money"
By Linda Stern, CBSnews.com, July 14, 2010

"Many have little to no savings as retirement looms'
By Matt Krantz, USA TODAY,   December   4, 2011

"Could taxes derail your retirement?"
By Liz Davidson, Forbes.com, February 2, 2012

"Fidelity: Couples Need $230,000 for Retirement Health Costs"
By Emily Brandon, USNews.com, March 31, 2011

"Today's Retirement Myth: A Million Dollars Is Enough"
By Selena Maranjian, The Motley Fool, January 15, 2012

Every month we see articles like this focused on the same issues. Is there anything new here? No.

What are they telling us?

FEDERAL PAYMENTS. Social Security and Medicare can not continue to make payments at the same levels in the same structure as today given the demographics of the United States. Is there anything you can do about this? No, you are powerless.   While Medicare collects an insufficient amount to sustain the majority of its spending, the Social Security Administration projects in its worse case scenario it will be able to pay 75 cents of every dollar projected. Not great but not awful either. MARKETING SLOGAN: HIRE A FINANCIAL PLANNER.

YOU MAY RUN OUT OF MONEY. While usually these articles focus on not saving enough they also raise the Bogeyman – disaster can strike at anytime. Your bad because you are not saving enough and even if you are saving enough something bad will probably happen to you. Just in case disaster strikes, save a cardboard box so you have somewhere to stay. Fear of the unknown and unknowable are not particularly inspirational. The upside is that those who are following the personal financial mantra of saving more and spending less can feel superior to someone else. "Thank goodness I own my annuity!" More on this later. MARKETING SLOGAN: BUY ANNUITIES.

YOU ARE NOT SAVING ENOUGH (AND YOU ARE SPENDING TOO MUCH). You are drinking too many lattes and will retire a pauper because of it. While frugality has its virtues, it is not an attractive alternative to your current lifestyle. Again while basic budgeting is valuable and we need to spend less than we make and set some money aside, the rules of thumb that get thrown around in these articles are something else. Do you have 6 months expenses readily available in cash – then you are financially irresponsible and doomed to live in a cardboard box (see above). MARKETING SLOGAN: BUY MUTUAL FUNDS.

TAXES. Even if you are saving enough we will confuse you with the complexity of the current tax code and, even better, the unknowable future tax code. Creation of complexity makes it so you won't dare to deal with this yourself but hand over your hard earned money to an advisor. MARKETING SLOGAN: TRUST A FINANCIAL PROFESSIONAL.

HEALTHCARE. Even if you are saving enough, you are going to suffer a long, painful death so you can either plan to save more or find an iceberg to float out on at a pre-determined time. One of the favorite numbers that gets thrown into these articles is you will need $250,000 for your health care costs (or more). The facts are that retirees spend on average between $4500-$5500 per year on healthcare costs depending on their age and general health conditions according to the US Bureau of Labor Statistics. Assuming you are retired for 25 years it is hard to figure where these numbers come from other than projecting unsustainable straight line projections. MARKETING SLOGAN: BUY LONG TERM CARE INSURANCE.

A MILLION DOLLARS ISN'T ENOUGH. What this really means is that if you do not have a Million Dollars, please do not bother a financial services professional. These articles assume that as a millionaire we are sitting around in tuxedos sipping brandy while our butler brings us the morning paper as if we were in some 1940's movie. The reality is fewer than 2% of people who will retire this year have $1million in financial assets. So what are the other 98% of retirees to do? The smart answer is not relying on a Financial Fee Extraction Industry professional. The reality is that retirement comes for these 98% and they find a way. MARKETING MESSAGE: PEASANTS NEED NOT APPLY – AFFLUENT AND MASS AFFLUENT ONLY.

OK, now that you are powerless, fearful, irresponsible, confused, and spurned, how are you going to prepare for retirement? After being beaten up, most people just give in and turn their money over to a Financial Fee Extraction Industry professional.

The Business Godfather offers you an alternative that is consistent with how other successful businesses are grown. My view is that as you build your Personal Financial Business, your focus should be on confidence, clarity and simplicity. We do need your effort and focus for a defined period of time but the goal is to provide you with freedom

What Charlie Brown's Parents Tell Us About Conventional Retirement Strategies

Save More and Spend Less is a common theme through articles like those listed above as well as throughout the personal financial industry. Remember the sound of the parents talking in all the Charlie Brown cartoons: Wahh, Wahh, Wahh, Wahh, Wahhhhh. Well that's the sound that most people hear when they hear the conventional retirement strategies telling them they need to Save More and Spend Less. Wahh, Wahh, Wahh, Wahh, Wahhhhh. You see, it's your fault you won't be able to retire. Wahh, Wahh, Wahh, Wahh, Wahhhhh. You may need to live in a cardboard box and eat oatmeal every day. Wahh, Wahh, Wahh, Wahh, Wahhhhh.

True as a business, we do want to periodically review our operating expenses to make sure we are getting value for what we are spending. At the same time, as a business, our goal is not to save money, but to make money. So yes, we need to spend less than we make but the amounts are more reasonable than you have been led to believe. The two areas that we are going to shift our focus to rather than saving more and spending less is Reduction of your Risk and Obtaining a More Consistent Rate of Return. Reducing Risk and Obtaining a More Consistent Rate of Return are the primary focus areas for institutional financial managers so this is where your focus should be as well.

As a business person, we would never enter a business where we took enormous risk with very little hopes of gain. However that is the approach to risk at the heart of the Financial Fee Extraction Industry model. Financial services institutions shift their risk to retail folks like you and charge you fees for the privilege.

Why No Rational Human Being Should Own a Mutual Fund

Mutual Funds were a great way for individuals to benefit from the stock market when barriers to entry were high:

information was scarce, fees were expensive, broker execution was slow, arbitrary and skewed against individuals and it was just plain hard to trade and invest. The advent of the Internet, the Information Age, the 21st Century, discount brokers and other innovations have torn down these barriers to entry for individual investors.

Right now there is no rational reason for anyone to own a mutual fund. I used to caveat that statement with unless you were required to by your 401K but now, most users of 401Ks have more options at their disposal to avoid mutual funds within their 401Ks. Additionally, as a consumer of the 401K you have influence over your HR department to provide more lower fee options such as Exchange Traded Funds. And if you are 59 ½, you are able to move these 401K funds into a self directed IRA which will allow you to focus your efforts on Reducing Risk and Obtaining More Consistent Return. Of course irrationality spurred by fear and perceived complexity are the glue that holds the Financial Fee Extraction Industry together.

The reasons why Mutual Funds make little sense have been known in the industry for years and are well explained by James O'Shaughnessy in his 1997 book, <u>How to Retire Rich</u>[1], which interestingly he used to promote his own mutual funds based on the strategies outlined in the book.

---

1 http://www.amazon.com/dp/0767900723/ref=rdr_ext_tmb

Mysteriously, with the explosion of information on the Internet these points are hard to find in more modern discussions of personal finance.

1. **FOLLOW THE MONEY**: Mutual Fund Managers are rewarded using an asset aggregation model rather than a performance based model, which leads to the motivation to amass large amounts of assets rather than to achieve outstanding performance.

2. **THE LAW OF LARGE NUMBERS**: Asset aggregation leads funds to grow in size which in turn makes it harder to find places to invest the funds capital effectively and even harder to obtain high percentage returns. For example, a $10 million fund that gains $5 million grows by 50% while a $1 billion fund that gains $50 million only gains 5%. The average Mutual Fund has about $1.5 billion in assets.

3. **STRATEGY CREEP**: The need to amass more assets and find places to put capital leads Mutual Funds to invest beyond their advertised or stated strategies. During the Internet Bubble bursting millions of "Value" Fund investors were surprised to learn that their fund managers had invested in all the hot growth stocks that were imploding at the time. The investors thought they were

protecting themselves but instead were undone by their mutual fund managers.

4. **WINDOW DRESSING**: At the end of every calendar quarter, Mutual Funds are required to provide a report to their investors that in part identify the Mutual Funds biggest holdings. It is common practice for funds to sell their low performers and replace them with the names of the high performers right before the end of each calendar quarter so the handful of people who actually read the report will say, "They underperformed but at least they had all the right stocks." Mutual Fund Managers chase performance of hot sectors so they effectively have a model of buying retail or at a higher price than they needed to – generally not an effective business or investment strategy. This is also a significant factor in Mutual Funds general failure to come close to the market returns.

5. **SELECTIVE RETURNS**: Why does every new or young fund have market beating returns? When fund companies start new funds they will fund multiple funds and only the winners will make it to the marketing campaign. Also in the marketing materials, the charts show the most favorable interpretation of their results. Unfortunately these high performers then revert to the mean

through underperformance as they are opened to the public and gain more assets.

6. **FEES**: At the end of the day, fees are what feed the Financial Fee Extraction Industry. One of my favorite slights of hand is when the fund shows a performance chart and then in super small type states "Excludes Fees & Expenses". We will show in the next section why you can not overlook fees.

There are other problems with mutual funds including the drag from not being 100% invested, to horrendous tax exposure, to horrendous transaction fees, to inexperienced, revolving managers.

The Financial Fee Extraction Industry recognized many of these limitations and as you can see in the accompanying chart[2], the number of Mutual Funds peaked in the year 2000 at around 8000 and has been dwindling over the years. One thing that has not dwindled is contributions to mutual funds – over $12 trillion and counting. Even as the markets have experienced a roller coaster ride and effectively zero growth in the 21st century, Mutual Fund assets have almost doubled. The reason this business continues to grow is that you keep sending your money in. Your Business Godfather's prescription is: **STOP SENDING YOUR MONEY TO MUTUAL FUNDS**.

2 Source Investment Company Fact Book 2011

Keep in mind, there are only about 6,000 or so investable grade stocks that these funds are allowed to invest in so we actually have more funds than stocks available to trade. This also undercuts most of the so-called advantages of funds. As the average fund has about $1.5 billion and the universe of investable assets is shrinking with private equity taking companies out of the public markets.

The most straightforward alternative is the established Exchange Traded Funds or ETFs. ETFs have been around for about two decades and like Mutual Funds offer diversification in broad baskets of investable assets. There are ETFs that track just about any investable asset from international stock exchanges, to global currencies, to commodities. While the number of ETFs have grown, most of the new entrants into the ETF world have some extreme disadvantages particularly those that rely heavily on derivatives like futures and options for their returns or those that have high fee structures. Your focus should be on high volume, low fee ETFs such as the SPY, which tracks the S&P 500 and the TLT which tracks the value of the 20 year bond.

For a fraction of a percent in fees, you will track the indices that the Mutual Fund managers have difficulty coming close to so you will beat 85% of Mutual Funds each year. The draw back is that you will be fully exposed to market risk. Later in this Guide, I will introduce you to some strategies you can use to reduce your risk and get more consistent returns than simple tracking the market indices.

More Fees, Fees, Fees, Fees, Fees, Fees, Fees Please

Before we get to Reducing Risk and Obtaining More Consistent Rate of Return we need to discuss fees. Fees are not an ancillary part of the Financial Fee Extraction Industry. Fees are the raison d'etre, lock - stock and barrel, hook - line and sinker, the whole enchilada – in other words everything that the Financial Fee Extraction Industry is about.

All the pictures of sunsets, yachts and beaches are designed to get you to hand over your assets so the Financial Fee Extraction Industry can feast on the carcass of your wealth and retirement plan. While I have no issue with industries that charge a fee for a valuable service, simple facts are that people are paying a premium fee for mediocre to negative returns. The US Securities and Exchange Commission identifies no fewer than 9 Fees related to Mutual Fund operations including Redemption Fees, Exchange Fees, Account Fees, Management Fees, Distribution Fees and Marketing Fees[3].

---

3 In the fee table, under the heading of "Shareholder Fees," you will find: Sales Loads (including Sales Charge (Load) on Purchases and Deferred Sales Charge (Load)), Redemption Fee, Exchange Fee, Account Fee, and Purchase Fee. (Although the fee table in Form N-1A does not specifically include "purchase fees," if a fund imposes one, it would be included in the fee table under this heading.) In the fee table, under the heading of "Annual Fund Operating Expenses," you will find: Management Fees, Distribution [and/or Service] (12b-1) Fees, Other Expenses, and Total Annual Fund Operating Expenses.

If you happen to hold those Mutual Funds in a 401K plan, then even more fees get extracted. USA Today Reported on 12-30-2011 "Many investors don't realize that more than a half a dozen fees may be charged against their 401(k) account for recordkeeping, administration, investment advisory, brokerage and management services. In addition, at least eight kinds of indirect fees and expenses could be charged. These are often shaved off the top of the account's investment returns." The US Department of Labor Identifies no fewer than 3 Fees related to 401Ks including Plan Administration, Investment Fees and Service Fees.

Now the most motivated of you have already pulled out your mutual fund quarterly report and found the "Expense Ratio" and are saying, "Well my fund only charges 1.5%." Keep in mind that the Financial Fee Extraction industry has lobbied hard against having to disclose all the fees they charge and currently the expense ratio does not include all expenses.[4] Investopedia reports 1.3 to 1.5% average management fees for stock mutual funds with a range of .2 to 2.0 %. The Investment Company Institute reports 2010 management fees had a simple average of 1.45%. Transaction fees represent another 1.44% on average and other fees can add another point or two to your expense line.[5]

---

4 http://www.investopedia.com/terms/e/expenseratio. asp#axzz2FbsZu72q

5 "Shining a light on 401(k) fee reports in 2012" by David Pitt; ETF Fee data from Morningstar.com, "The Real Cost Of Owning A Mutual Fund" by Ty A. Bernicke, http://www.investopedia.com/university/mutual-funds/mutualfunds2.asp#axzz1k1D7qZaV, http://www.icifactbook.org/fb_ch5.html

These are just numbers but let's bring this into reality. Mutual Funds are fond of making straight line projections that show a beautiful sloping arc assuming that you get average returns of 7% a year. In fine print they always say excludes fees and expenses. Of course we know that the markets never provide straight line returns but this is a standard rubric used so we will use it to examine the power of the financial services fee structure.

Effectively the Financial Fee Extraction Industry has become a partner in your Personal Financial Business with no risk and little accountability for results. While its silly and unrealistic to use straight line projections to discuss market returns, because this is a standard rubric used by the Financial Fee Extraction Industry the following tables demonstrate the enormous extent.

The following charts assume you start with $100,000, invest for 30 years at a constant rate of return and compare the results to those you would receive had you used the SPY ETF to track market returns or if you used a 50-50 balance across SPY-TLT to replicate a balance between stocks and bonds. Reality tells us we will not get a constant rate of return but focus on the percentage of gains you would sacrifice at the altar of financial services fees and expenses.

In the first scenario, we apply the average Annual Management fee of 1.45% and see that over 30 years, 28% of your gains get paid to the Mutual Fund managers.

Effectively the Mutual Fund Managers are using your capital to benefit with little risk to themselves.

	Opening Balance	Fees*	Ending Balance	Percentage of gains paid in Cumulative Fees
Average Mutual Fund	$100,000	1.45% (.0145)	$505,530	28%
SPY ETF S&P 500 Stocks	$100,000	0.09% (.0009)	$740,170	1.6%
SPY ETF & TLT ETF	$100,000	0.12% (.0012)	$736,062	1.9%

Only includes Annual Management fees – excludes other fees for mutual funds.

This table compares the same scenario but adds in the average 1.44% transaction fees incurred by Mutual Funds to manage your money. In this case 60% of your returns are chewed up in fees and expenses.

	Opening Balance	Fees*	Ending Balance	Percentage of gains paid in Cumulative Fees
Average Mutual Fund	$100,000	2.99% (.0299)	$306,202	60%

Only includes Average Annual Management Fees and Transaction Fees – excludes other fees for mutual funds

But remember, 85% of mutual funds fail to match the market each year. While many miss market returns by a wide margin, this next table assumes they miss by only 1% annually. By doing less well, your partner get even more of your gains – 70% in this scenario.

	Opening Balance	Fees*	Ending Balance	Percentage of gains paid in Cumulative Fees
Average Mutual Fund	$100,000	2.99% (.0299)	$231,045	70%

Only includes Average Annual Management Fees and Transaction Fees – excludes other fees for mutual funds

Even better, let's layer on a 1 % fee to your Financial Advisor or your 401K administrator. In this scenario, 78% of your gains are paid out in fees.

	Opening Balance	Fees*	Ending Balance	Percentage of gains paid in Cumulative Fees
Average Mutual Fund	$100,000	3.99% (.0399)	$169,305	78%

Only includes Annual Management Fees, Transaction Fees and a 1% Advisor/401K fee – excludes other fees for mutual funds

What masks these meager returns is that you keep sending money every month, because you are doing what you have been taught to do by the Financial Fee Extraction Industry.

Have you ever interviewed the people you are sending all these fees to? Have you ever conducted a background check on the people you are trusting with your money? So you have handed your money over to a stranger who you have never met and never will meet. How confident are you that this stranger will be looking out for your best interests? Will you know when the stranger isn't looking out for your best interests? While I am in favor of being kind to strangers, do you really need to keep giving them all your money?

You carry all the risk, provide all the capital and receive very slight benefit from being involved in these transactions. As a business person, does it make any sense for you to participate in transactions like these?

Very simply NO, NO, NO, NO!

Afraid of Outliving Your Money – Welcome to Annuities

The fear tactic most commonly associated with selling annuities is the fear that you will outlive your money and will need to live like a pauper. Annuities are contracts that provide periodic income with complex and customizable provisions. Some annuities provide fixed payments for a period of years or for the life of the beneficiary. Some annuities have variable components linked to the stock market. While annuities are not as prevalent as Mutual Funds, they represent a large portion of income for the Financial Fee Extraction Industry.

Annual fees for annuities are generally more than for mutual funds starting at 2% per year. Annuities also have high upfront fees or surrender charges ranging from 2-10% that come right off the top that represent the initial sales fee for the annuity. The reason the sales person is so passionate about annuities when talking to you about them is that they pay the best.

Because annuities are a high fee income vehicle, it never makes sense to use an annuity as a savings vehicle during the accumulation phase of your long term wealth plan. There are however times during decumulation - meaning when you are spending your money - where an annuity, even with its high fees, can be useful for you. Annuities can be used to provide you with a fixed income for a certain set of years or to ensure a base level of income is always available to you, particularly as you get older.

As with all things, simple is usually better. The more complex your annuity is – the more features, bells and whistles it has – probably means you are paying for something you do not really need.

Why Are You Saving For Retirement?

Every personal finance site has some form of retirement calculator where you tell it how much money you have, when you want to retire and how much money you want to make in retirement and POOF it gives you a magical answer. They usually have some Rule of Thumb that you should target 80 % of your pre-retirement income (or more).

One thing we all have learned the past few years is that life is not a straight line so these calculators are not particularly useful. Moreover, retirement is not some big number but a combination of a number of factors related to where you live, your quality of life, your health needs, your family needs and your desire to leave a legacy of your life and accomplishments. These are actually fairly straightforward calculations you can make now.

We know that most people do not retire as millionaires. They go through retirement A Little Poor but OK – what I call the A.L.P.O. Imperative. Back in the early 1980's, news shows would regularly have a piece on how social security was not paying senior citizens enough and that they were forced to eat dog food. These continued stories eventually got President Reagan and Congress to raise the Social Security tax collected as well as the payouts from Social Security into close to its current form today.

Most people who have contributed to Social Security regularly will have enough to cover their basic living expenses – groceries, gas and incidentals. Remember for all the people afraid that Social Security won't exist keep in mind that every country has some form of financial support for the elderly. The worst case scenarios project only 75 cents on the dollar will be available – still enough for basic living.

The complexity comes when we add in other factors such as to what extent you choose to become the Bank of You, Relive Sins of the Past, Your Lifestyle, Your Need for Capital Goods, Your Healthcare Needs, and Your Desire to leave a Legacy. Most of these relate to value choices or your current state of affairs.

What I mean by the Bank of You, relates to what extent you feel obligated to pay for your family weddings, vacations, education, cars, homes and other expenses. There are some people who will have certain things they see as a personal obligation to their families and other people who will say "Not my Problem." You need to take this into account in identifying whether you need a strategy to address this.

Reliving Sins of the Past mainly relates to debt. If your house is paid off and you have no debt you don't need to worry about this. If you do have debt maybe you need a plan to eliminate this debt prior to retirement or with a specific timetable within retirement. Perhaps you downsize your house and move to a less expensive place. You need to account for this when calculating how much you need in retirement.

Your lifestyle is a big component of your retirement income need as you move from being A Little Poor but OK (A.L.P.O.) to traveling the world, golfing every day and eating out at restaurants regularly. If that is part of your plan you need to account for it in your overall retirement income needs. Remember, you still need a basic budget so you spend less than you make.

Now Capital Goods are something easy to overlook but are probably the most predictable. If you own a house, every few years you are going to need to paint it, replace the furnace, put on a new roof, etc. If you drive a car you are probably going to need multiple vehicles in retirement. I think across the board this is the most overlooked aspect of retirement budgeting but it is also the most predictable. You probably need about $1000 per month to address this aspect of your retirement.

Healthcare is totally dependent on you. If you are generally healthy, eat right and exercise, guess what? Your expenses are going to be lower than average and possibly even negligible overall. If you have a chronic condition, your healthcare expenses are going to be higher than average and you will need to address this in your retirement income projection and have a strategy to address it.

The Desire to leave a Legacy is the last stop. Once you have everything else covered, this can represent a significant motivation for your retirement program and may need some attention.

Each person is going to have a different answer for each of these areas. As you work through these areas you may realize your income need in retirement is not that great. OR ... you may discover you need some serious attention given to your overall plan. In either case, let's get started.

Rapunzel, Rapunzel, Let Down Your Hair: Options Inside the 401K Prison

Many people have a significant part of their wealth tied up in 401K plans or the Government equivalent, Thrift Savings Plan (TSP). They have 3 basic options for controlling their Long Term Wealth Assets:

1. For people over 59 ½, they generally can shift any and all of their 401K and TSP balance into an IRA which allows them great flexibility, fee reduction as well as a full range of strategies focused on reducing risk and obtaining more consistent returns.

2. For people under 59 ½ that are no longer employed by the company that provided their 401K or by the Government provider of the TSP, they can shift any and all of their 401K and TSP balance into an IRA which allows them great flexibility, fee reduction as well as a full range of strategies focused on reducing risk and obtaining more consistent returns.

3. For people under 59 ½ that remain employed by the provider of their 401K or TSP, their options are more limited.

For those of you stuck in this third category you can do more than just pine away for that magical day when you turn 59 ½.

We can start with a Fee Reduction strategy. Many of these 401Ks and TSP plans offer what are call Lifecycle funds where you pick a date you would like to retire and magically a big pot of gold awaits you. Unfortunately the reality is that these offer rotation between the stock and bond portions of your 401K and TSP choices, for a fee of course on top of the fees that you already are paying within the individual funds. Steer clear of these heavy fee, low reward opportunities.

You should review each of your fund choices and focus on their Expense ratio as well as their annual turnover. The higher the annual turnover, the higher your hidden trading expenses will be. If you can find low cost alternatives then you want to look at the risk component of the fund.

Since Benjamin Graham's Intelligent Investor recommended periodic portfolio rebalancing, rebalancing has been a bedrock of financial advice. As assets have become more correlated some studies indicate there is limited benefit to portfolio rebalancing. You can use a straight 50-50 rebalance between stocks and bonds or an overweight rebalance of 60-40 or 75-25 no more than once per quarter.

In your savings strategy, you should generally make your contributions to ensure the maximum match from your employer. As your income increases, the deferral of income from tax also provides an incentive to use these programs. If there is no match or to the extent your contributions exceed the match you should allocate some of what you should have saved to an IRA that provides more control and the opportunity to reduce your fees.

Most business owners are not trapped in someone else's retirement program so keep in mind, you have great flexibility in what you and your employees can invest in.

There are three basic types of retirement plans that you can use for your business: IRA Based, Defined Contribution and Defined Benefit.

Selecting between the 3 relates to how much income you are looking to put into Tax Deferred and Tax Free opportunities on an annual basis. This relates to how much of your available income are you spending versus saving. Most business owners I have worked with are comfortable with lower levels of contributions because they spend most of their available income, however, as we start growing our Personal Financial Business we can really magnify our opportunities.

Defined Benefit Plans: Maximum Contributions, Maximum Regulations

Defined Benefit plans for the most part are holdovers from the 20th century when higher margin businesses with lower wage rates and lower employee turnover could put excess capital to work in a defined pension based on certain events occurring. For a single owner/ handful of employees business or a family owned business these may still be appropriate to establish if you generate a lot of excess cash and want to reward all your employees/owners with significantly more than $50,000 per year in tax deferred compensation. For a high employee turnover business, they can also be a source of value creation for the owners assuming very few individuals other than the owners will actually be around to claim the benefits. For the most part however, there are more cost effective and more efficient ways to generate returns and benefits for the owners than the constraints, structures and costs required to fund, manage and maintain defined benefit plan funds and the plan itself.

Defined Contribution Plans: Most Bells and Whistles Including Tax Free Option

Defined Contribution plans include formal Profit Sharing plans and 401K plans and are the most common formats used by medium and large businesses. With the recent inclusion of the Roth 401K option as well as the addition of the Total Contribution limit between Employee and Employer at 25% of wages up to $53,000 in 2016, Defined Contribution plans can also make sense for small businesses.

401Ks, like IRAs, can invest in a broad spectrum of assets beyond stocks and mutual funds. 401Ks can invest in real estate, tax liens, precious metals, currencies, options, private companies and futures. This is where you as a business owner can identify multiple wealth management strategies and implement them in a tax deferred or tax free fashion. You also need to evaluate which of these assets make sense for a tax deferred or tax free vehicle.

For example, real estate is generally better held in a taxable account rather than tax deferred due to all the deductions associated with real estate ownership available to offset current income and the ability to defer taxation in appreciation through not selling and 1031 exchanges. However, real estate that you are flipping, rehabbing with intent to sell or if you have identified real estate with a high likelihood of appreciation (not sure where this might be) could be a great fit for a tax free account.

Precious metals present another example where the asset may not be appropriate for a tax deferred account because a bar of gold just sits there and does not generate income. Effectively it already is tax deferred and you have total control over when the taxable event might occur. On the other hand, a tax free account could be appropriate if you will be trading in and out of positions or if you are expecting significant appreciation.

One of the attractions for many retirement plan options is the ability to reduce your current tax year income and therefore current tax liability by putting your contributions into a tax deferred plan. You will owe taxes whenever you withdraw the funds but presumably that will be in the future and possibly you will be in a reduced tax bracket.

The Roth 401K option allows you to put in post-tax dollars but all your gains and contributions can be withdrawn bracket. once you are 59 1/2 and the plan has been open for at least 5 years. If this is included as an option in your 401K you and your employees can split the annual employee contribution ($18,000 with $6,000 additional for folks over 50 for 2016) between either tax deferred and tax free accounts. The power of tax free income can not be overstated.

While establishing a Roth IRA has certain income restrictions, these income restrictions do not apply to a Roth 401K. The Roth 401K does have Required Minimum Distributions at age 70 ½ like a traditional IRA or 401K plan. However, after the age of 59 1/2, you will be able to transfer your Roth 401K into a Roth IRA to avoid the Required Minimum Distribution requirements and for even greater flexibility in your investment activities and choices.

The concept of the increased amount for Total Contribution limit between employees and employers allows for 401Ks to provide as much benefits as SEP plans by allowing the employee to contribute up to $18,000 and the employer to contribute the balance up to $53,000. Basically this allows a 401K plan the ability to include contributions in the same amounts as a SEP IRA plan. For a small company with a single or handful of employees, this might be an attractive option to beef up your retirement savings.

Best I can tell, the maximum for Tax Free contributions is the Employee amount of $18,000 in 2016 but other than the IRS guide there is little discussion on this available. As stated earlier, the minimum recommendation for a tax free account is $10,000 but the more you are willing to pay in taxes today, the more likely you will be better off tomorrow provided you understand how to generate income on a consistent basis from your tax free accounts.

On top of all this, 401Ks (tax deferred or tax free) can provide the option of generating a loan against the proceeds held in the account as well which might be attractive for flexibility and access to your funds.

When selecting your 401K, you need to understand the fees and the fiduciary duties you have as the plan sponsor. The fees vary wildly from provider to provider and can be fairly significant. Even more mysterious is asking the service provider what you get for the fees paid and you will be told something on the order of provide the plan (form they already produced), manage the plan (electronic preset with payroll) and help in selecting what to invest in (which also pay the provider) so effectively you pay on an ongoing basis for upfront services.

One of your challenges will be to find a 401K provider that is not solely a front for mutual funds or a stock broker so you can access a broader range of investments as allowed by the IRS. For a single owner business, you are looking for what is known as a "Solo 401K." This provides the ability to put in the maximum amount for your benefit as well as use the proceeds for loans.

The fiduciary responsibility of having a 401K requires that you make "prudent decisions" regarding selecting a plan and a financial advisor. For a Solo 401K this is not much of a concern as you will be the primary beneficiary but if your plan applies to more people then paying the fees associated with plan management may be worthwhile.

IRA Based Plans: Low Cost & High Flexibility

IRA Based Retirement plans include those that have traditionally been focused on small business such as the SIMPLE and SEP Plans. Prior to the 21st century revisions of the 401K rules, IRA based plans provided the lowest cost and highest flexibility option for small businesses. IRA based plans allow the same broad range of options available in a 401K as discussed earlier including real estate, tax liens, precious metals, currencies, options, private companies and futures.

SIMPLE stands for Savings Incentive Match Plan for Employees and allows for a mix of Employee and Company contributions. One limitation on SIMPLE plans are that they can be the only plan your company makes available whereas other options generally allow you to provide multiple plans. The SIMPLE plan provides the lowest contribution amount available to employees ($12,500 in 2016), which is why they are usually not the most attractive option.

SEP stands for Simplified Employee Pension and represents the best option if you want the company to be responsible for all contributions. This allows for up to 25% of compensation or $53,000, whichever is less, in 2016 and effectively puts the funds in an IRA that each individual can manage on their own. A uniform percentage needs to be applied for owners and employees.

SEP Plans require less reporting than 401Ks and are significantly lower in cost than 401Ks. They do not however have the tax free, loan or salary deferral options available in 401Ks. Basically it is a giant traditional IRA with out the ability to convert to a Roth. This will build your Tax Deferral wealth.

Retirement Plan Summary

SEP Plans provide the simplest, most straight forward way for you to build a Tax Deferred wealth strategy.

401Ks with the Roth Tax Free Option provide the most flexibility including the ability to develop both Tax Deferred and Tax Free wealth strategies.

Defined Benefit Pension plans provide a way for single/family owned and operated businesses to maximize tax deferred compensation. If $100,000 or more is available annually per owner for tax deferral and you want to maximize your tax deferral strategies, this may be a good option as well provided that owners provide most of the services or if you have a high employee turnover business.

Other than the SIMPLE plan, you can combine multiple plans to provide access to multiple benefits.

21ˢᵗ Century Investment Strategies

As we develop our sources of funding for our Taxable, Tax Deferred and Tax Free Income strategies, the next step is to identify which strategies will reduce your risk, help you get more consistent returns and allow you to take advantage of today's best opportunities.

The problem that the Financial Fee Extraction Industry and all of its clients (you) have run into in the 21st century is that the US based stock model that they rely on has not provided much in the way of real returns and has produced negative returns when you apply the Financial Fee Extraction Industry model. Effectively, the S&P 500 in January 2013 is at the same level as it was in 2007 and 2000, the dawn of the 21st century. From this Zero percent return, recognize that the vast majority of mutual funds failed to do this well and for that they charged you 1-4 % per year in various fees and then incurred an additional 1.44% per year in transaction fees. What has cushioned your statement from feeling the full brunt of this is that you have kept shoveling money in to your accounts which have covered your fees and hopefully kept you treading water – although I know for many they still have not recovered from the Credit Crash of 2008 and even the Internet crash of 2001.

The Chart below highlights the differences between the late 20th century market that the Financial Fee Extraction Industry needs to cover the costs of its fee extraction model versus the actual market we have experienced and will continue to experience for much of the next decade. In order to build your retirement in the 21st century, you need to take advantage of the best opportunities and accept the world as it is, not how you would like it to be.

	20th Century Investor	21st Century Investor
Goal	Capital Appreciation	Capital Preservation & Appreciation
Responsibility	Experts	Self
Diversification	Portfolio Diversification	Targeted Diversification
Markets	U.S.	Global
Instruments	Mutual Funds, Stocks, Bonds	ETFs, Stocks, Options, Forex, Futures, Bonds
Strategy	Buy & Hold	Active Management
Use of Capital	100% Invested	Opportunistic
Optimal Market Condition	Make Money When Market Goes Up	Make Money When Market Goes Up, Down or Sideways

GOAL: The Financial Fee Extraction Industry Model is based on the assumption that the market goes up at a nice consistent rate of return. Every Financial Services website includes a Retirement Calculator which will provide you with a projection of the growth of your funds at a consistent rate for the rest of your life. Unfortunately, we know that life is not a straight line and neither will be the returns you get in the market. All the mantras of the Financial Fee Extraction Industry Model are designed to get you to expose yourself to market risk so you can maximize your capital appreciation opportunity in a single market: Buy and hold – always be fully invested – dollar cost averaging - you don't want to be out of the market – you can't time the market. In the 21st century, the Financial Fee Extraction Industry Model has exposed its victims to enormous risk for very little gain.

As a business person, you would never accept a business with enormous risk for very little gain. In your Personal Financial Business you should never accept enormous risk for very little gain. The 21st century requires you to start applying the same business acumen you use in your everyday business to your Personal Financial Business.

In the 21st Century, we have learned that our first order of business is to preserve our capital and take capital appreciation opportunities when they are available. The first part of capital preservation is realizing when a particular market has peaked and taking profits off the table. The second part of capital preservation is realizing that when a particular market has peaked, the money will flow from that market into a different market and being able to move capital between different market opportunities will not only reduce drawdowns but will also increase opportunities for capital appreciation.

Capital preservation is essential for every business especially your Personal Financial Business. If you opened a restaurant and hired the greatest chef in the world, how long would you be in business if you did not preserve your capital? A couple of months, maybe? Not long, that's for sure. For your Personal Financial Business, you have kept it afloat by shoveling more money into it. Let's start treating your Personal Financial Business like any other business and focus on capital preservation.

Responsibility

Much of the Financial Fee Extraction Industry based news and information is put forth to make things seem complicated and inaccessible so you believe you need an expert to succeed. TV is filled with experts; newsletters tell you they are experts; your funds tell you they are experts.

The reality is with the advent of electronic trading in the 1990's, with the information explosion available via the Internet, the financial services business like every business has moved to a more cost effective, self service model. The ability for you to manage your money effectively has never been better.

Moreover, what we have learned in the 21st century is that the only person looking out for you is you (and the Business Godfather). Just like you have in the rest of your life, take responsibility for your Personal Financial Business.

Diversification

Don't put all your eggs in one basket is a well known axiom to support diversification. Recognize however, diversification is a concept not a strategy. Diversification is not a wealth management strategy or income strategy. What we want to do is diversify very focused approaches for income, for wealth management, for wealth creation and for wealth preservation. For each strategy, we want to put all our eggs in one basket and watch that basket very carefully as Andrew Carnegie has taught us. Commit to a strategy and execute it.

Having a balanced portfolio is purported to be safe but this comes from an individual company stock perspective. There is enormous risk associated with holding individual stocks. Diversification across individual stocks is for people who are willing to accept this risk – for most people individual companies represent more risk than necessary for a less than stellar return. We can achieve diversification by holding single instruments relating to broad markets such as Exchange Traded Funds that track the S&P 500. Some people hold multiple Mutual Funds in the name of diversification without realizing the Mutual funds hold largely correlated assets. What makes the application of diversification to mutual funds more absurd is that there are more mutual funds (8000) than tradable stocks (~6000) available in the US.

We will use diversification by targeting the best opportunities and focusing on them. If we stick with stocks, we can use stock sector rotation to identify the 2 or 3 likely next areas of opportunity. We can use the relationship between stocks and bonds to overweight our portfolio based on whichever is the dominant asset at that time. We can use the correlations between assets such as the dollar and oil or the seasonal characteristics of certain commodities as we target our focus on the best opportunities available. My preference is to identify Plan A, Plan B and Plan C to achieve a particular Income or Wealth Management objective and then implement those.

Markets

The story of the 21st century has been 3-4 Billion people saying I want in to the world economy – China, India, Brazil and other emerging markets. Globalization has impacted every industry and has provided great opportunities in Global stock markets while the US market has provided a roller coaster ride and is largely where it was at the start of the 21st century. Growth in the US and Europe is likely to be no better than slow and steady as we digest the excesses of the credit bubble and aging populations. Because growth is the primary thing that stock markets are designed to reward we need to go where the growth is. If we are going to be in stocks, we need to adjust our orientation to more global opportunities rather than just US based stocks.

Instruments

As stated earlier, we need to move beyond mutual funds and not solely rely on stocks and bonds for our Personal Financial Business. FOREX or currency is the life blood of the global economy and provides us with some of our best opportunities for income, wealth and purchasing power protection. Futures let us access every major market including commodities essential for global growth such as gold, oil and food. Moreover, as we carve out time to implement our Personal Financial Business FOREX and Futures provides us with nearly 24 hour access 5 days per week rather than being subject to the schedule constraints of the US stock market.

Strategy, Use of Capital and Optimal Market Condition

In order to succeed in the 21st century, you will need to abandon the Financial Fee Extraction Industry Model with its discredited buy and hold, 100% Risk exposure and capital appreciation reliance and adopt an active management approach to look for the best opportunities in whatever market conditions are presented to you. Just like you do in your everyday business.

How well are you positioned to take advantage of global macro-trends in your Personal Financial Business?

As mentioned earlier, the story of the 21st century is globalization. The lifeblood of the global economy is FOREX or currency that fuels international trade. FOREX is a superior instrument for learning how to trade because we can access this market at just about any time that fits in our schedule with a small account as we master order execution and risk management in live market conditions with mini and micro lots. FOREX provides superior opportunities for income and can also be used for wealth management and growth. Instead of having your money in the S&P 500 since 2001, if you had your money in Australian dollars you would have more than doubled your money.

I love the Australian dollar because it tells us whether growth is happening in Asia particularly China and India. Even if we are not going to trade the Australian dollar, over the past few years it has been one of the leading indicators of what was going to happen in the US stock market. The Australian Dollar is tomorrow's newspaper for opportunities and can help us Obtain More Consistent Returns, as we understand what it tells us about global market opportunities.

We can also use currencies beyond income and wealth management and use it as a purchasing power preservation vehicle. One of the dirty little secrets of the 21st century is the erosion of the purchasing power of the dollar. That's a problem if most of your wealth is denominated in US dollars. If one of your wealth preservation strategies includes cash, instead of having those dollars in a currency that is a victim of globalization like the US dollar you can hold equal amounts in three different currencies such as an Asian Currency (Japanese Yen or Australian Dollar), a European Currency (Euro, British Pound or Swiss Franc) and a commodity currency (Canadian dollar, New Zealand dollar or Australian dollar). Along with your US dollar exposure, these three currencies will rise and decrease with the waves of the global economy. At the moment you need to make a major capital purchase such as a car, a vacation or house repairs – use whatever currency is the strongest at that time. There are US based banks such as Everbank that allow you foreign currency exposure with the same FDIC insurance that applies to other US based banks.

As you learn more about FOREX or Currencies, you may never need to own another stock again.

Deflation and Inflation

Whether we have deflation or inflation, we can get on the right side of this trade or be a victim of it. Getting on the right side of this trade will probably have the most impact on your wealth over the next several years. Because we have been trained with an inflationary bias, due to our inflation based economic teachings and memories of the late 1970's and early 1980's, most people are very concerned with inflation while we have been experiencing great deflation across our assets and in our economy. The Federal Reserve has been telling us for 5 years that they are unconcerned with inflation and are trying to slay the deflationary dragon.

Rather than turn this in to a philosophical debate or an economics lesson, the more important question is how do we get on the right side of this trade? Futures, Options on Futures and ETFs provide us with opportunities to benefit from Bond and interest rate opportunities in either direction. Currencies, FOREX futures, options on FOREX futures and ETFs allow us to protect ourselves from US dollar depreciation in any form. Physical commodities like gold and oil offer similar protection and many ways to access their power through futures, FOREX, Options or ETFs.

At least one of your wealth management strategies and at least one of your wealth preservation strategies should be incorporating deflation and inflation strategies so you are not a victim of the 21st century.

Risk Diversification Through Income

As we model our Personal Financial Business after banks, trusts and insurance companies, we will reduce our risk and get a more consistent rate of return by selling options on a consistent basis. First we need to figure out what rate of return we want and then select an instrument that can provide us with that rate of return with less risk than through outright ownership. Cash secured puts are a vehicle where a rate of 2-12% per year is achievable with broad based assets with significantly less risk than outright ownership. Basically, your cash becomes your reserves, just like an insurance company.

If we do hold assets we can use options and futures to protect ourselves against a drop in price of the asset we hold. Options and Futures allow you to customize your insurance of your assets. Very powerful and certainly essential if you are going to be managing your Personal Financial Business.

Further Research

For more information about the Active Investor and Business Godfather methodologies, please visit:

www.activeinvestor.us
businessgodfather.com
plantonotpayyourtaxes.com

To learn firsthand from Chris how to plan to not pay taxes, sign up for one of his webinars today.

Webinar Discount Code: PTNPT20

To learn more practical strategies to increase your business wealth, check it Chris Koomey's bestselling book, <u>The Business Godfather Treatment</u>, available on Amazon. com:

https://www.amazon.com/Business-Godfather-Treatment-Streetsmart-Handbook-ebook/dp/B01ATUL9B4

Also follow us on social media:

LinkedIn: **https://www.linkedin.com/in/chris-koomey-493b2a2**

Twitter: @bizgodfather

About the Author

Chris Koomey started his first business when he was 19 and since then has opened up businesses and helped others open up and grow business as a business owner, business consultant and business attorney. Chris helps growing businesses in fields ranging from education to technology. Chris graduated from the Marshall Wythe School of Law at the College of William and Mary after receiving BA & MA degrees from the University of Chicago and an MS degree from George Mason University. He lives in Arlington, Virginia, with his wife and family.

35372781R00077

Made in the USA
Middletown, DE
01 October 2016